Above The Glamour

To Joe

I Hope you enjoy the book!.

Jo Kere

Above The Glamour

Regina Keiser, Richard Daub

2008

Above The Glamour

Contents

Acknowledgement

To: Natalie Korsavidis—For all your editing assistance.

To:　　　*Doug, Kirsten and Kelly—Because of you, I am.*

To:　　*The dedicated Flight Attendants—Especially the crews of Flights AA 11 and 77, UA 173 and 93, AA 1291 and AA 587. Memories of you will always fly with us.*

I.

The Hijacking

Ken, this is Jean," I said into the phone as calmly as I could, but my voice was quivering and my hands were shaking. "The prisoner has a gun to my head. He wants you to come back here. He says we're going to Havana. Ken, this is no joke—this is for real!"

Even as I spoke these words, I couldn't believe it was really happening.

"Jean, we don't have enough fuel to go to Cuba," the captain responded. He was already aware that we were being hijacked, having been informed by one of the other flight attendants moments before I called the cockpit. I put my hand over the receiver and repeated to the hijacker what the captain had just told me.

"I don't care if we don't have enough fuel to go to Cuba!" he yelled. "I don't care if I take this plane down! I'm serving eight consecutive life sentences, and if I go, you'll go with me! You tell him if I don't see this plane turning, you're a dead woman!"

"Ken, you have to turn this plane towards Cuba *now*!" I yelled into the phone. "If you don't do it *now*, he will shoot me! Turn the plane *now*!"

"Okay, Jean, calm down. Tell him to look out the left window and he'll see that we're turning."

I told him to look out the window and he did.

"Tell him I want to speak to him," the captain said.

"He wants to speak to you," I said to the hijacker, and he grabbed the phone from me.

"I'm Ishmael Ali LaBeet!" he said loudly into the receiver. "Do you know who I am? I'm the Fountain Valley Murderer!"

"I know who you are," the captain said. "Mr. LaBeet, we're a little short of fuel and I really don't feel that we have enough to make it to Havana."

"Don't be shitting me, man!" He was yelling again. "You have enough!"

"Mr. LaBeet, would it be alright if we stopped for additional fuel?"

"Don't give me that low-on-fuel shit! We're not landing anywhere but Havana—or the sea!"

⚓

I had started the day in a good mood. It was New Year's Eve, 1984, and my husband Doug and I had plans to attend a party later that evening. I was really excited because it was going to be the first time that we would be going out since having our daughters, Kirsten and Kelly, ages four and two. I had lucked out getting this trip because I had been flying night trips all month, but flight 626 from St. Croix to JFK would land early enough to allow me to go out later that night.

For this flight, I was assigned to be the 'number one' flight attendant, also known as the 'purser.' The purser is in charge of the flight and is the one who makes the announcements, fills out the paperwork, acts as the liaison between the cockpit and the rest of the crew, handles problems with passengers if the other crew members can't, and other various duties. Also, if there's a problem during a flight, the purser is the one called into the supervisor's office to explain what happened.

During boarding in St. Croix, I was informed by the agent that there would be three U.S. Marshals on the flight. The passengers and crew alike were in a festive mood, and everyone was looking forward to going home to begin their New Year's celebrations. Our only real concern was that there was a weather advisory in New York that might cause us to be delayed or diverted. Otherwise, everything seemed fine and we took off right on schedule.

We had been in the air for about an hour when the number six flight attendant called me. I was working the first class section at the front of the aircraft while she was working the second section of coach in the back.

"Do you know who the prisoner is?" she asked me.

"What prisoner?"

"The prisoner-you know the one the marshals brought on board."

"I was never informed that we were transporting a prisoner!"

"He's the 'Fountain Valley Murderer'!"

"Oh-well, I don't know who that is."

His name was Ishmael Ali LaBeet, a native of St. Thomas and a former soldier with the U.S. Army who had fought in Vietnam. In 1972 he was the ringleader of what became known as 'The Fountain Valley

Massacre!. He and four other men shot eight people to death at the Fountain Valley Country Club, a ritzy resort in St. Croix that had been popular with wealthy foreigners. After robbing everyone in sight, LaBeet opened fire and the others followed suit. Their guns had been stolen from the property room of a nearby police station. They initially got away and fled into the hills, but were caught several days later after the largest manhunt in the history of the Virgin Islands. Despite being cold-blooded killers, these five black men would later become symbols of racial injustice when they claimed that they had been tortured into giving confessions by white police officers after being taken into custody. They also became heroes to some native islanders who felt oppressed by a local government that catered to the wealthy foreigners.

The following year, they went on trial and prominent civil rights lawyer William Kunstler volunteered to represent one of the defendants. His association with the case turned the trial into an international media circus. The Black Power movement used the spotlight to promote their cause despite the men having long criminal histories and that three of the people murdered at Fountain Valley were black (two of them were employees of the country club and the other was an electrician's helper on a job assignment there). The five defendants were eventually found guilty, and each was sentenced to eight consecutive life terms in prison.

LaBeet was sent to Lewisburg Penitentiary in Pennsylvania and had been serving his time there, but was in St. Thomas to testify in a civil court case related to the abuses he and his accomplices allegedly suffered while in custody after the shootings. Unfortunately for me and the rest of the crew, American Airlines flew him from St. Thomas to St. Croix, which is where he boarded flight 626. I did see LaBeet board the plane at around the same time as the marshals, but since nothing was said about him, I didn't realize that he was their prisoner. His outfit of a sport shirt and slacks had him blending in with the rest of the passengers.

"Well, that's interesting," I said after I was given the lowdown. I had never heard of this guy before or 'The Fountain Valley Massacre.' While what he had done sounded horrific, it happened such a long time ago that it didn't seem real to me and I didn't worry about it. Besides, he was in the custody of three marshals-he was their problem, not mine. I had more important things to worry about. I didn't have time to worry about murderers.

Sometime later, the number six flight attendant called me again to tell me that the prisoner kept getting up to go to the bathroom. The marshals would then go in and check the lavatory *after* he had already been in there. Looking back now, it is clear to me that they should have been checking the lavatory *before* he went in, but at the time I assumed they knew what they were doing. There was a rule back then that guards transporting a prisoner had to remove the prisoner's handcuffs before takeoff so that his hands wouldn't be encumbered in the event of a crash-but these guards took it a step further and had removed his cuffs before he even got on the plane! He basically had free reign to get up and go to the bathroom unescorted whenever he wanted, but the thinking was, *Where's he going to go? He can't escape while we're up in the air!* For all I knew, he could have been going to the bathroom because of something he ate. Prison food probably wasn't that great, so it wouldn't have surprised me if his digestive system was all out of whack. It didn't occur to me that he might be searching for a gun that had been planted in one of the two lavatories at the back of the plane. He wasn't sure which lavatory it was and was having difficulty finding the gun.

When we were an hour outside of New York, one of the other flight attendants came up front and said that the marshals wanted me to page for a doctor because the prisoner wasn't feeling well.

"You have got to be kidding me," I said. By now I was tired of hearing about this guy, and if I paged for a doctor, that would mean I would have to fill out an incident report and do all this extra paperwork because I was the number one flight attendant. I didn't want to stay a second longer than we had to after landing at JFK.

"What's his complaint?" I asked.

"He's complaining of stomach pains."

As a mother, I knew there wasn't a whole lot you can do about a stomach ache.

"I'm not paging a doctor for a stomach ache," I said. "He probably just has gas or something. I'll go check it out myself."

The aircraft was a DC-10 and the seats were divided into three sections: first class in the front of the aircraft and two sections of coach in the middle and rear. The prisoner and the marshals were sitting in the last rows in the rear section of coach. Since it was such a big plane, it took me a little while to get back there. When I got to the second section of coach, a passenger sitting in the front row stopped me.

"Go away!" he whispered anxiously. "The man has a gun!"

In the back of the section, I saw this man ordering the marshals to get on the floor. He appeared very nervous and agitated, and you could hear a pin drop in the cabin. Before I had a chance to do anything, he turned and saw me.

"You!" he yelled, pointing his gun in my direction. "Get over here!"

Coach seating in a DC-10 was set up in a 2-5-2 configuration, which meant that each row had two seats on either side of the plane and five seats in the middle. The last row of the section was up against a wall, and behind the wall there were two lavatories and exit doors. There were two aisles that led to the back. I was standing in one while the hijacker was in the other. There was a walkway in front of the first row of seats where I was standing, so I could have just walked directly over to the other aisle and then headed straight to him in the back, but for some reason I decided to walk to the back via the aisle I was standing in and then cross over. To this day I'm not sure why I did this—I think at that point my mind had not fully comprehended the situation and needed a little extra time to figure out what was happening. I also knew that he wouldn't be able to see me when I was behind the wall. Fortunately, the hijacker didn't seem to notice that I was taking the long way, and when I got to the back I stopped, leaned against the wall, closed my eyes, and said to myself, *I can't believe this is happening...*

I had been trained for situations like this, but never in my wildest dreams did I think it would actually happen. It was surreal. I don't know how long I stood there, it couldn't have been very long because I knew that he'd come looking for me if I didn't appear soon. At some point, I eventually took a deep breath and said to myself, *Okay, let's just do it.*

As soon as I got there, he pointed the gun at my head and said, "You're mine for the night. I want you to take me to the cockpit."

"Well," I said, "if you let me—"

"I want to go to Cuba and I need to go to the cockpit now!"

"It'll be a lot quicker if you just let me call them!"

In the meantime, the other flight attendant had followed me to the second section of coach a short time after telling me about the prisoner's stomach ache. Fortunately, the hijacker didn't notice her because he was too busy pointing his gun at me while I was making my way to the back of the aircraft. When she saw what was happening, she immediately turned around and hurried to the cockpit to inform the captain. When I called up there and told them, the captain was already aware that there was a situation in the back.

Our captain was Ken Korshin, an experienced pilot and a flight standards supervisor for American who had about 20,000 hours of flying time logged. Ken was as cool under fire as they come. He thought that he had been through it all while at the controls, but this was new to him. He still managed to keep his cool, and after finding out that the hijacker wanted to go to Cuba, he and flight engineer Hal Tiedemann immediately assessed the fuel situation. Normally we wouldn't have had enough fuel as the company standard at the time was to fill the plane with only as much as needed for that particular trip unless there were circumstances that made it absolutely necessary to put in extra. Since there was a winter weather advisory in New York as well as our alternate landing site in Boston, Hal insisted that the tanks be topped off in St. Croix. Even with the extra fuel, however, it was going to be close. We were only forty-five minutes outside of New York after leaving from St. Croix and were now going to turn back and fly three hours in the opposite direction to Havana. The assessment in the cockpit was that we should be able to make it, barely, but the captain didn't want the hijacker to know that. He knew that almost anything could happen when a U.S. aircraft entered Cuban airspace and was hoping to convince the hijacker to land somewhere else.

After the hijacker finished yelling at the captain, he slammed down the phone and ordered me to summon the rest of the flight attendants to the back of the plane. Fortunately, he either forgot his demand for the captain to come back there or was satisfied that we were really on our way to Cuba because he didn't mention it again. This was very fortunate since one of the last things you want to happen in a situation like this is for the captain to leave the cockpit and risk having something happen to him.

Since the flight was only about three-quarters full, the hijacker had the other flight attendants sit in the last two rows with the marshals, who were sitting there quietly. He knew exactly how many flight attendants were on board and seemed very familiar with the aircraft, which made me wonder how long he had been planning this and how much help he had had.

After the other flight attendants were seated, the hijacker ordered me to make a P.A. announcement to the passengers with his instructions for them. After he told me what to say, I spoke calmly into the handset and said,

"Ladies and gentleman, we have a passenger, a Mr. LaBeet, who has taken command of this aircraft and we are now on our way to Havana, Cuba. He has requested that you remain in your seat, cross your hands on the seatback in front of you, and watch the movie, which we will begin again shortly. You are to remain like that until further notice. If you need to use the restroom, you must raise your hand and wait for permission, and you are not to close the lavatory door while you are in there." Without hesitation the passengers did exactly as they were told, and I remember thinking that I wished they were always this compliant.

No one tried to be a hero, not even the marshals, who were as well-behaved as the passengers and did not say a word during the entire ordeal. While all the other flight attendants were sitting in the last two rows, the hijacker made me sit in the jump seat where the flight attendants normally sit during takeoff and landing. He stood over me with the gun pointed at my temple the entire time. He eventually calmed down once he felt that everyone was cooperating and that he was in full control of the situation. Occasionally he would become belligerent, like when the phone kept ringing and I offered to answer it.

"It's probably just the cockpit calling us for a cup of coffee," I said. "They're always bugging us to bring them coffee."

"You are not to touch that phone!" he said.

"Well, it's really not a big deal to bring them a cup of coffee."

"I don't care! I'm gonna kill the captain, and I'm gonna kill you too!"

"Why? Why are you going to kill him? And why are you going to kill me? You don't even know me!"

"Because you stand for everything I hate. You're blonde, white, and materialistic."

"I don't know how you can say that. I have two kids and I'm working my butt off—"

"I don't want to hear about your kids!"

Realizing that talking about my life would only make him angrier, I quickly changed the subject and started asking about his life. This seemed to calm him down a little and he told me about growing up in St. Thomas and that he had seven sons by five different women.

"What's the matter? Can't make any daughters?"

He just looked at me and I worried that my attempt at humor might have angered him, but his expression seemed more defiant than angry.

"I will," he said calmly, "in Cuba."

"I have two daughters," I said.

"I don't give a shit about your daughters!," he yelled.

I quickly changed the subject again and tried appealing to his vanity by saying that he seemed like a smart guy and asked him if he read a lot of books in prison. He said that he had been studying accounting while at Lewisburg, which surprised me because I couldn't picture him poring over a ledger while punching numbers into an adding machine. I managed to keep him engaged in conversation while being cautious not to say something that might anger him. After doing this for nearly two hours, I couldn't think of anything more to talk about. Fortunately, my fellow flight attendants picked up on this and started talking to him. Having overheard our entire conversation, they knew by now what subjects to avoid. They brought up very safe topics such as what it's like to be a flight attendant, what other jobs they've had, what they might be doing if they hadn't become flight attendants, and so on.

While they were talking, I started drifting into the realization that I might never see my family again. *Oh my god, the girls—they're so little! Oh my god...*I started to cry, but I quickly realized that I had to get a grip and not think about my family again until this was over. That would only cause me to lose control which wouldn't help any of us and might even upset the hijacker. Instead, I started thinking about a friend of mine who was also a flight attendant for American. She had this saying that she used whenever we were having a bad flight: *This too shall pass.* So I called upon this saying and told myself, *This Too Shall Pass. Either I'm going to walk off this plane and be alright or I'm going to die. Either way, this situation is not going to last forever. It is going to end.* And it worked.

The flight seemed to last an eternity. The captain eventually announced that we would be landing in Havana in about thirty minutes and for the crew to prepare for landing. The hijacker would not allow us to get up, so we were not able to prepare the cabin for landing. The cockpit crew was in the dark about what was going on in the back since the hijacker wouldn't let us talk to them. They just did their best to follow the normal procedures. The cabin was pretty much prepared anyway since we had already started getting ready to land when we were approaching New York. There were still some unsecured carts left out which can be very dangerous during landing since they are extremely heavy and can cause serious injuries if they go flying through the cabin.

After the captain made his announcement, the hijacker became very nervous and told me to get up because we were going to the cockpit. I stood up and he jammed his gun into my back and we headed down the aisle towards the front of the plane. When we got to the cockpit, I stood between him and the captain, who was talking to Havana's air traffic control tower requesting increased airspeed for landing because we were running low on fuel. They responded with a negative, but the captain turned to the first officer and flight engineer and said, "Well, we're going to do it anyway because we're flying on fumes right now."

The cockpit became real quiet after that. The captain got back on the radio and told air traffic control that they couldn't see the runway lights. It was dark and the lights of Havana were visible through the haze, but there was a dark spot on the landscape about fifteen miles ahead where the airport should have been. The flight engineer said something about looking at the chart and reached into a portfolio that was on the floor next to his seat. Suddenly the hijacker yelled, "Keep your hands where I can see them!" The engineer yanked his hand out of the portfolio and slowly raised both of his hands above his head to show that he did not have a weapon.

"Proceed with what you were doing," the hijacker finally said.

About ten miles outside the airport, first officer Scott Chamier got on the radio and said, "Havana, this is American 626 — would you please turn the lights up?"

There was no immediate response, and he and the captain looked at each other. A few moments later, the runway lights finally blinked on up ahead and somebody in the cockpit exhaled a breath of relief.

"Mr. LaBeet," the captain said, "would you mind sitting down and fastening your seat belt?"

The hijacker did not respond.

"I don't want you to fall when we land," the captain said.

There was still no response.

"If you don't sit down, please at least brace yourself against the seat. I don't want you to fall and have that gun go off."

The hijacker still didn't say anything, but he did grab hold to the back of the captain's chair and braced himself just before we touched down. I had taken a seat and buckled up and looked out at the runway lights ahead. I wasn't used to having such a good view when we landed.

Despite coming in at a higher speed than normal, the landing was relatively smooth, though the runway itself was a little bumpy. Because we were going so fast, it took a while to slow down and we stopped an inch or two from the marshes at the end of the runway. There were already emergency and police vehicles parked on the tarmac with flashing lights and the hijacker had ordered the first officer to radio the tower and tell them that he was *a political prisoner from the U.S. Virgin Islands seeking asylum in the People's Republic of Cuba.* The person at the other end didn't seem to understand at first. The first officer handed the microphone to the hijacker and he repeated his request in Spanish. A few moments later, someone on the other end radioed back and said they understood.

At this point, he became really fidgety and he asked me how to get to the baggage compartment. I told him I didn't know, but was thinking that I was probably about to find out. He then pressed the gun to my head and told me to get up. As I was doing so, I leaned over the flight engineer's shoulder and said, "Listen, if I don't make it, tell my husband and my kids that I love them."

"Don't worry," he said. "I'll take care of it."

I thought for sure that I was about to die.

After leaving the cockpit, we stood near the forward door and he didn't seem to know what to do next. Ground personnel had brought over the ramp stand. This is the staircase used to board and deplane the aircraft when there isn't a jet bridge at the terminal.

For some reason, the ramp was brought to the second door, instead of the front door, where we were actually standing. This was peculiar because the front door would normally be used for boarding and deplaning.

I'm one of the most honest people in the world. I never lie. But if ever a situation called for a little white lie, this was it! I said to him, "They're not bringing the stairs to this door, they're bringing them to the next one—you have to let me go because I'm the only person on this plane who knows how to open the doors." Of course, all the flight attendants know how to open the doors—that's one of the most important functions of our job, especially during an emergency! But he bought the lie and ordered me to go over to the other door, open it, and then come right back. My thought was that he intended to keep both myself and the captain as hostages and was serious when he said earlier that he was going to kill us both.

The door he was standing in front of was by the first class section next to the cockpit. The second door where they had brought the stairs was behind the wall that separated first class from the first section of coach, so he couldn't see what was happening. When I got there, another flight attendant had already opened that door and there were Cuban police officers demanding to know where the hijacker was. I told them he was up front and warned them that he had a gun. They stormed right into the first class section anyway. In the meantime, the other flight attendant and I ran to the back of the plane in case anyone started shooting.

When we got to the back, we found the rest of the flight attendants wearing their life vests. I was a little confused and asked them why they were wearing their life vests. The flight attendants said that they weren't sure if we were going to make it all the way to Havana or if we were going to have to ditch into the water because of the fuel situation. The possibility of ditching had totally slipped my mind since I was more concerned about the gun pointed at my head. Later we found out that every U.S. Coast Guard vessel and cruise ship in the area had been positioned óff the Cuban coast just in case we had to ditch. A U.S. fighter jet had been dispatched with a four-star general on board just in case Cuba did not receive us on friendly terms.

We didn't know what was happening up front. I called the cockpit and told them that we were in the back and that we weren't coming forward until we got word from them that all was clear. Fortunately, the Cuban police were able to apprehend the hijacker without any shooting and promptly took him away. To this day, American flight 626 is his last official known whereabouts. U.S. law enforcement agencies don't know what happened to him after he was taken off the plane. Articles have been written in Caribbean newspapers about how he is still at large in Cuba and has been seen walking the streets of Havana.

After he was gone, we were just happy that he wasn't our problem anymore and that nobody had gotten hurt. The captain made an announcement that the individual had been removed from the aircraft. I remember taking a deep breath and saying, *I still can't believe this...* The passengers were then taken off the plane and bused to the terminal. This is when the reality began to sink in that we were in Cuba and at the mercy of Fidel Castro.

After the passengers were gone, the flight attendants and the cockpit crew had a briefing in the first class cabin.

"Don't think for one minute that I don't know who the real hero is," the captain said. "All we did was fly the plane. Jean, whatever went down here tonight, you did an amazing job."

Besides the extra fuel in our tank, another thing that had worked to our advantage that night was that Fidel Castro happened to be in a good mood. He agreed to fuel us up and let us go without a hassle. Perhaps it was because it was New Year's Eve; the anniversary of the night former Cuban dictator Fulgencio Batista fled the country in 1958 and allowed Castro to take power. Who knows what he would have done with us if he was feeling cranky? For all I know, he could have just thrown us in prison and kept us there as long as he pleased.

As it turned out, however, we couldn't have been treated any nicer— the Cuban people were just absolutely wonderful! We were allowed off the plane and went into the terminal. As if we landed from an ordinary flight, we did some shopping in the gift shops and were given a free meal at one of the restaurants at the airport. I can't recall what I had to eat or if I even ate anything at all because my heart was still racing. I do remember thinking that I was missing the New Year's Eve party back home and how I would much rather have been there than, sitting in a restaurant at the Havana airport.

After dinner, the flight attendants and cockpit crew were escorted back to the plane, where we had another briefing. The captain informed us that he and the flight engineer were going to make a flight plan and then the Cubans were going to release us.

"We have the right to go to the first U.S. port of entry," he said, "which in this case would be Miami. But I'm going to leave that up to Jean. Where do *you* want to go, Jean? Miami or New York?"

"Without a doubt," I said, "we're not going anywhere but home!"

The captain and the engineer went to work on the flight plan while the passengers were being bused back to the plane. After the flight plan was finished, the captain informed the F.B.I. and the F.A.A. where we were going and a short time later, we departed with one less passenger. One of the flight attendants asked the marshals why they hadn't done anything. They just shrugged and said, "What could we do?" The way it turned out, however, it was probably better that they were such wimps. If they had tried something, they may have gotten all of us killed.

When we were in the air, I made an announcement to the passengers that we didn't have any food supplies. We left out some carts and they were informed that they were welcome to help themselves to whatever beverages we had. By now we had been on duty for over twenty hours and were exhausted. We had reports to do and just needed to chill out. The passengers seemed to understand this and were really good about leaving us alone! They were wonderful and truly grateful that things ended up so well. There was one girl, however, who was upset because it was her sixteenth birthday and she had missed her sweet sixteen party. She cried all the way back to New York. All I kept thinking was *you'll have plenty more birthdays after tonight, honey. This could have ended up a lot worse than it did...*

Three hours after departing from Havana, everyone on the plane got excited when the lights of the New York skyline came into view, and a cheer went up after the plane touched down at JFK. As the passengers were deplaning, they kept thanking us and telling us what a great job we did and wishing us a happy new year. Never have I seen so many people just happy to be alive.

In the meantime, the jet bridge was packed with people—American Airlines officials, F.B.I. agents, F.A.A. reps, N.T.S.B., Customs, N.Y.P.D., airport security—you name it, they were there. After all the passengers had deplaned, the crew was escorted into a crowded conference room where each of us was assigned one F.A.A. rep and one F.B.I. agent. We had only been there a few minutes when a man came in and started calling my name.

Oh great, I thought. *Now what?* I got up out of my chair and identified myself. The man asked me to follow him.

What I hadn't thought about yet was what was going on at my house during this whole ordeal. It turned out that once air traffic control got word that a hijacking was in progress, representatives from the airline started calling the families of the employees on the flight to let them know what was happening. When they called Doug, he thought it was a joke. My younger brother was constantly playing jokes on me. He would often call in the middle of the night saying he was crew schedule and telling me to report to the airport immediately. Another time, our car had been stolen from the train station, and I was livid that the police couldn't do anything about it. He called one Saturday morning pretending to be a police officer and invited me down to the station to pick out a new car since they weren't able to find our stolen one! Since we had plans to see him later that evening at the New Year's Eve party, Doug assumed he was playing another joke! Especially since the part about going to Cuba seemed so far-fetched.

"You know," Doug said to the American Airlines rep on the other end, "I have a brother-in-law who is constantly playing jokes like this."

"I assure you, Mr. Keiser, this really is American Airlines and we do not joke about matters such as this. We just want to make you aware of the situation before you see it on the news."

Doug is normally a very calm person and usually never loses his cool. When he did realize that this was not a joke, he needed information that they did not have. He told them he was going to the airport, but since this was the era before cell phones, they advised him to stay home. This way they could contact him there when they had more information. Doug called my mother and asked her to come over and watch the kids. He told her that I was having car trouble and that he had to pick me up. If he had told her that I had been hijacked, she probably would have had a heart attack!

After my mother got to the house, Doug raced out to JFK and found the terminal already packed with reporters. After a while they started approaching him and asking if he was waiting for someone on the hijacked flight. He kept telling them that he wasn't. When more and more people started showing up, they stopped bothering him and started bothering other people.

When my plane finally landed, security wouldn't let anyone near us. When they told Doug that I was being taken to a conference room and that he couldn't see me, he very calmly said to them, "I need to see my wife right now to see that she's okay. And if you don't let me through, I'm going to start talking to these reporters."

A few minutes later they let him through. That's why I was called out of the room. He kissed me and said that he just needed to see that I was okay. When I saw that he was crying -and Doug never cries -I started crying too.

"I can't do this right now," I said. "I'm okay, I'm okay, I just have to talk to these people now-but wait, who's with the girls?"

I felt better when he said that my mother was with the girls and that he had told her I was only having car trouble. Afterwards, I went back into the conference room and spent several hours talking to the F.B.I. and the F.A.A. representative. We filled out reports and finally around five or six in the morning, they released us.

Doug insisted that we drive home together. I wanted take my own car so that I wouldn't have to come back the next day to pick it up. Usually, I would be able to win an argument, but not this time. Doug just said, "Jean, you are not going to win this one, so just get in the car with me and we'll worry about your car another day."

When we got home, the kids were just getting up. It was really tough to just walk in the door and act like nothing happened. The phone started ringing. By then everyone already knew about my flight being hijacked. People were calling all day and coming over. I had to keep telling the story again and again. The next day the crew was required to go back to the airport for meetings with American Airlines officials who had flown in from corporate headquarters in Dallas, Texas. I had to tell them the same story over and over, as well.

Finally, a few days later, things started to calm down. I had only a few days off to recover before my next scheduled trip, which was the following Sunday. I could have used several weeks or even months off after that night. American's philosophy at the time was that an incident like this was merely part of our job and that the best thing we could do was get right back up in the air; like people who fall off horses!

The Saturday before my next trip was really tough. I didn't know what to do. I kept asking Doug, but all he kept saying was, "Jean, I can't tell you what to do. I will stand behind whatever decision you make. If I tell you to quit and then down the road you're sorry that you did, then it's my fault. If I tell you to keep working, you will feel that I want you to keep working because I like the money your paycheck provides. So I'm not going to tell you what I think you should do. Whatever you decide is fine with me."

I did know, however, that I was strong. I should be able to overcome what I had been through. I was scared that something like this might happen again, but I was also angry that the hijacker, this lowlife murderer, had control of my life for those few hours. I really liked my job. If I quit because of what he did, it would be like letting him control the rest of my life. Finally, I decided to go to work and see what would happen. If I was alright with it, then fine. If not, then I would have a decision to make.

That next trip included the same leg as the hijacked flight, St. Croix to New York on a DC-10. That didn't exactly set my mind at ease. I was happy to find out, however, that one of my girlfriends, Susan, had called crew scheduling and insisted on working the trip with me . That made me feel a lot better. The whole crew I worked with was great and very supportive. Many co-workers and friends had sent me cards. Everybody kept telling me what a great job we did and were in awe of what had occurred. It meant the world to me that my co-workers showed how much they cared; especially when all the airline did was throw us a small luncheon several months later!

For the first time, however, I did start to think about how my family would be affected if they were to lose me. The day after the hijacking, when everyone was coming over to the house, I tried to downplay the story and left out the more dangerous parts if the girls were within earshot. I didn't want them picturing a crazy man holding a gun to Mommy's head. I was more concerned about Kirsten because she was four; Kelly was only two, which I didn't think was old enough to really understand what had happened.

About three weeks later, however, I was scheduled to work a flight that had a 5:00 AM sign-in. In the middle of the night Kelly had woken up vomiting. She was very ill and I got up and changed her sheets and took her into bed with us. By the time everything settled down, I had been awake for most of the night. Kelly was between us. I looked at the clock and said to Doug, "Great, now that I've been up all night, I have to get up in an hour to go to work!"

Right after I said that, Kelly lifted up her head and said, "Mommy, will there be a man with a gun again?"

I just looked at Doug in disbelief. We already knew that Kelly was an extremely perceptive child, but I could not believe that she understood what happened well enough to be worried about it. That's when I realized that her being worried was all that *I* really needed to understand. I looked at her sweet face and assured her that the bad man would not be on mommy's plane ever again!

As for the job itself, I was fine after that first flight back until about two months later when I was scheduled to work a flight from New York to St. Croix. The crew was informed that we would be transporting a prisoner! I was in the number one position again. After the prisoner was on board I pulled one of the marshals to the back of the plane and asked him what the guy was in prison for.

"Murder," he said.

"That's it!" I said.

I stormed into the cockpit and said, "Don't let them shut the door because I'm going down to flight services to let them know that I'm not working this flight. You'll have to get another flight attendant." Without waiting for a response, I stormed out of the cockpit and back into the terminal.

Flight Service wasn't very understanding. All they said was, "Okay, just get your bags and go home." That was fine with me, even if it meant losing my job. I wasn't going to work another flight with a prisoner on board.

While I was in the flight service office, the other flight attendants explained to the captain why I had stormed off. On my way back to the plane to get my bags, the captain was waiting for me on the jet bridge.

"Jean," he said. "You went flying out of the cockpit so fast that you didn't even give me a chance to respond." I was shaking. He put a hand on my shoulder. "If this prisoner isn't here, can you do this flight?"

That possibility hadn't occurred to me.

"Oh, well, yes," I said.

The flight service manager was now standing there as well. The captain turned to him and said, "Jean stays, the prisoner goes."

They took the prisoner off and I worked the flight without a problem. Since then, American has implemented much stricter regulations regarding the transporting of prisoners. Now a prisoner has to remain handcuffed throughout the entire flight. If they want to eat, the guards have to feed them and they're not allowed to go to the bathroom. Despite these changes, I will not step foot on a flight in which a prisoner is being transported. Nor will I fly on New Year's Eve. It now seems unthinkable that there was once a time when prisoners were free to roam the cabin of a commercial aircraft; especially when cockpit doors were not secured and anyone could just wander in and take control of a flight. How naive we were!

Months after the hijacking, I received a call from an American Airlines representative who told me that I needed to come to the airport. There was an F.A.A. man that wanted to talk to me. It was 9:00 in the morning. It was snowing and the girls and I were still in our pajamas. The last thing I wanted to do was drive all the way out to the airport and talk to yet another F.A.A. representative. I had been doing this for the last two months.

"I don't have anything left to say," I said to the person on the other end. "Tell him to look in my reports. It's all in there."

"I know, Jean," she said. "But you still have to come."

"Well, what am I going to do with the girls? I don't have a babysitter. I'm tired of disrupting my daughters' lives every time someone wants to talk to me"

"You know what, Jean? Bring the girls! We'll watch them for you. He said it wouldn't take that long."

"Alright," I said. "I'll be there in about an hour-and-a-half."

After hanging up with the airline representative, I called my best friend, who was also a flight attendant, to see if she wanted to have lunch when I was on my way back home from the airport. She was away on a trip, but her husband answered the phone. He was a New York City cop and I told him about being called out to the airport. He said to me, "Jean, if this F.A.A. guy wants to talk to you that badly, let him come to your house. Why should you have to take the kids out on a day like today?"

"That's not a bad idea," I said. So I called the airline back and spoke to the woman who called me earlier. I told her "I'm not saying that I won't talk to him, but I would prefer if he came to my house."

"Well, I don't see that to be a problem," she said. "We can get him a rental car. Just give me directions."

After hanging up with her, I realized that not only did I have to get dressed, I also had to dress the girls, vacuum the house, make the beds and run out and buy coffee cake! The man showed up right after I got back from the store. I asked him to take a seat in the living room and told the girls to go play downstairs while Mommy talked to this man. Kids are curious creatures, however, and a little while later they came up to see what was going on. I introduced them to the man and then sent them back downstairs. Naturally, they came back up again. The F.A.A. man said he didn't mind. He asked them how old they were, what their favorite toys were, and said silly things to make them laugh. He just absolutely fell in love with them. They liked him too because at one point they ran downstairs and brought back their favorite dolls to show him. A little while later, he said to me that he didn't have any more questions. He thanked me for my time, apologized for any inconvenience, and then headed back out into the snow.

I thought this man was just another F.A.A. guy who had just another report to fill out. Months later, I received a letter stating that he had nominated me for the F.A.A. Gold Medal of Extraordinary Service. I would be receiving only the third one ever given out in the fifty-year history of the F.A.A. at that time.

There was a black-tie ceremonial dinner in Philadelphia. The man who had come out to the house on that snowy day gave a speech in my honor. He also told me why he nominated me. He said, "We deal with cockpit crews and flight attendants all the time, and sometimes we just see them as airline personnel. When I was in your home and saw that, in addition to saving the lives of over two hundred people on flight 626, you were also the mother of those two beautiful little girls. I just had to nominate you for this award."

After I received the award, things finally settled down. It didn't take me long to realize that the best way to deal with the bad is simply not to think about it afterwards and just move on. That's all you really can do. Of course, it's impossible not to think about the bad things once in a while. Sometimes when I'm driving to work I allow my mind to wander and the memory of that night floats by. I still get angry about what that hijacker did, how by hiding behind that gun he was able to seize control of my life and the lives of every other person on board that plane. But after the anger surfaces, I remember that there are better things to think about like my family, my friends, my co-workers, and how I didn't allow that horrible man to take from me the career that I truly loved.

2.

Below The Glamour

I was seven years old when I realized what I wanted to do with my life. It was during a trip with my family to spend the summer with relatives in Germany. We had emigrated from there when I was one. It was the first time I remember ever leaving New York and it was very exciting. We traveled by plane, which in 1959 wasn't as common as it is today. Back then, ships were still the most popular way to get to Europe and flying was a very extravagant, elegant way to travel. People got really dressed up to fly. I remember wearing my Easter dress and my older brother wore a suit. My mother had on this beautiful chiffon dress that was just absolutely stunning. My baby brother was only one at the time. The four of us together looked like the picture-perfect modern family making the bold leap into the jet age.

Our flight was booked on TWA to depart from Idlewild Airport (the former name of JFK) with a stopover in London. I remember the announcement being made that our flight was going to be delayed for several hours. I didn't mind so much because just being at the airport was exciting to me. After a while though, it felt like we had been there forever. At one point, my father ran home and got us some blankets so we could sleep right there in the terminal. Finally, they announced that our flight was going to begin boarding. Since this was before there were jet bridges, we had to go to the gate and then out to the tarmac, where we climbed the stairs to board the plane.

At the top of stairs, we were greeted by a tall, pretty stewardess wearing this beautiful blue uniform with matching hat and aviator wings pinned to her coat. She looked down at me with a big smile and said hello. I was just awestruck. Right then and there, I knew what I wanted to be when I grew up. I wanted to be a pretty lady just like her and wear a pretty uniform and jet set all over the world and meet all the interesting people who flew on airplanes. It seemed like such a glamorous lifestyle. From that moment on, it was all I ever wanted to do. It's funny to think how a single random moment can have such an impact on your life.

Shortly after takeoff, my baby brother made a mess in his diaper that left a stain on my mother's dress. These were the days before Huggies and my brother had on a cloth diaper that soaked right through. My mother became very upset. Not only was her dress ruined, but the clean diapers were in a suitcase that had been stowed in the baggage compartment. The stewardess came over with some damp cloths and was very nice about helping to clean up the mess. That should have been my first clue as to how glamorous this job *really* was, but I was too busy admiring her uniform and hair and makeup to even notice what she was doing!

When we got to London my older brother disappeared in the terminal just before our flight to Germany was supposed to begin boarding. My mother once again became very upset, but I was too absorbed in the scene to share her panic. It was exciting to be so far from everything I was used to and to notice the subtle differences of the people and things compared to back home. I remember looking at the departures and arrivals board and seeing the names of all the different places, many of which I had never heard of and some that I couldn't even pronounce. Each destination an exotic new world waiting to be discovered. I hardly noticed that my brother was missing, but my mother did eventually find him in time for us to make our flight. While my mother was upset with him for running off and he was upset for getting into trouble, I was having the time of my life!

In all it took sixteen hours to get to Germany, and it was those sixteen hours that set the course for the rest of my life. It was a truly amazing summer visiting our relatives and seeing the countryside and eating all that wonderful German food. What I remember more than anything else about that trip is the pretty stewardess who greeted us on the plane in New York. Little did she know what an influence she would have on one little girl's life!

After graduating high school, I applied to several of the major airlines, but I quickly found out that you had to be twenty-one or at least twenty-and-a-half before they would even consider hiring you. I had already waited so long to graduate high school and start flying only to find out that I was going to have to wait at least another two years. I was so disappointed and spent a long summer trying to figure out what

I was going to do for those next couple of years, and after not being able to think of anything else, I finally enrolled at Nassau Community College in the fall.

Two years later I earned my associates degree. I was hardly enamored with the college scene and wasn't really interested in continuing on to a four-year school. The classroom I was seeking was inside the cabin of a commercial airliner racing across the sky at 400 M.P.H., not some musty old room in a brick building covered with ivy.

I started applying to the airlines again, but none of them were hiring due to the fuel crisis that was going on at the time and flights schedules were being scaled back. Once again, I became very frustrated and began to wonder if it was ever meant to be. For the past thirteen years, my mind had been so fixated on becoming a flight attendant that it was very difficult to imagine doing anything else. I wasn't ready to give up my dream! In the meantime, I had to find something else to do.

I eventually found a job working in the personnel department at Sky Chefs in Manhattan which was the catering division of American Airlines. It turned out to be a very interesting position, and my co-workers came from different backgrounds and cultures. After becoming familiar with my position I actually enjoyed working there. I was in charge of temporary personnel. I had to dispatch temporary employees to the departments where employees were either sick or on vacation. I interviewed non-management applicants and college kids looking for summer jobs. I took new hires on tours of the catering facilities at the local airport and facilitated exams.

The best part of the job, however, was that I had travel benefits with American. I was able to fly on weekends and holidays and at least get a little taste of being up in the air. After a while, I started flying less and less because I was simply too tired. The nine-to-five lifestyle was not what I had expected it to be, especially since I had to commute on the train from Long Island into Manhattan and then take a subway to the office. This took well over an hour each way. Here I was working Monday through Friday and living for the weekends, but when the weekends came I was too exhausted to do anything. I was twenty-one years old and dying to get out and see the world, but instead I was stuck sitting in an office and riding trains all week. On the weekends, all I could do was rest and recover so I would be able to do it all over again the following Monday!

Late that fall, the airlines started hiring flight attendants again. Since I was already an employee of American Airlines, I was able to put in for a transfer rather than having to go through the whole hiring process. This meant that I would fly to Dallas and meet directly with the head of flight attendant training without having to first be interviewed by several middle managers like outside applicants had to do.

The minute I walked into the office in Dallas, I felt very welcome. The man who interviewed me was very nice and friendly and I felt very much at ease talking to him. Afterwards, I left with the impression that it had gone really well. Still, you never know! Being this close to my dream and then having to wait to hear if I was accepted was agonizing. If this didn't come through, I would be devastated.

Two weeks later, the letter came to the office in New York via board-mail. I sat at my desk staring at the envelope. I was afraid to open it because I knew I would start crying if I hadn't been accepted. I was going to take it into the ladies room and open it in there, but my boss walked by before I had a chance.

"Well, Jean," he said. "It's *the letter*."

"I know," I said. "I think I want to open it in private. I'm going to take it to the ladies room and open it in there."

"What, are you kidding me?" he said and snatched the envelope from my hand. He tore it open, dropped the letter on my desk, and said, "Good-bye."

I looked at the letter and then back up at him.

"I already knew," he said with a big smile. "I called Dallas right after you did the interview and asked them what they thought. I knew you were accepted two weeks ago!"

"Why didn't you tell me?" I cried.

"I thought it would be better if you found out the official way."

I was engaged to Doug at the time, and he was just as happy about the news as I was. A couple of weeks later, however, I received another letter saying that the January class that I was enrolled in had been cancelled indefinitely. The airlines had started cutting back flights again and they wouldn't need any new flight attendants in the near future. There was no timeframe for when training would resume. For now I was stuck at Sky Chefs doing the nine-to-five routine.

Doug and I got married in May 1974. We took a three week honeymoon. We traveled to Hawaii, then to Germany to visit my grandparents. They were too old to travel and hadn't been able to attend our wedding. After Germany we spent a weekend in Aruba before returning home. It was a wonderful time and I wished that it could have lasted forever. Going to work that first Monday morning was a challenge. Besides the letdown of the honeymoon being over, I wasn't ready to go back to riding the Long Island Rail Road trains an hour into Manhattan every day and then stepping into subway cars that reeked of urine and garlic just so I could sit behind a desk for eight hours and then have to go through it all again in order to get home. This was not what I wanted to do with my life. So, when I got to work that morning, I went right into my boss' office and gave my two weeks notice. I told him that I just didn't like working in the city and commuting on the trains. He said he understood but asked me to stay at least until they found a replacement. I agreed to do so under the condition that I could leave when I had a job interview scheduled.

During my lunch hour, Doug called and asked how my first day at work as a married lady was going.

"It's going great," I said. "I gave my two weeks notice!"

He was surprised at first because I hadn't said anything about quitting, but he knew how I felt about working in the city. He fully supported my decision and was very understanding. I am sure he was wondering if I was one of those women who got married just to quit their jobs! Even though I was happy with my decision, I also knew that I was right back at square one with my career- or lack of it!

Several weeks later, I landed a job at the TWA Ambassador Club at LaGuardia Airport. I was excited about it at first because I could now drive to work instead of taking the train. Unfortunately, driving to work was the only thing I liked about the job! They didn't know what they wanted me to do. They trained me to do just about every different job at this club. I didn't get to do any one thing long enough to really learn what they were trying to teach me. I greeted people, announced flights, bussed tables, answered phones, served drinks—I did a little bit of everything and a whole lot of nothing. And the people who worked there were just awful. They acted like they didn't want anything to do with me and all they really seemed concerned about was getting good tips from the high rollers who came in to their club and ordered expensive drinks before catching their flights.

By my fifth day, I couldn't take it anymore. That day, I drove all the way out to LaGuardia to go to work, but I couldn't bring myself to get out of the car. I just sat in the parking lot watching the planes take off wishing I was up there instead of on the ground. I looked over at the TWA terminal and thought, *I hate this job*. After sitting there for an hour, I finally just started the car and headed home. When I got back to the house, I called TWA and resigned!

My next job was at Seaboard World Airlines, which was a cargo airline at JFK. This job lasted three days. I was under the impression that I would be doing secretarial work for their vice president. That was fine with me at the time because I really had no idea what else I wanted to do. When I got there, I discovered that they wanted me to do computer programming. This was 1974, when computers filled entire rooms and most people had never even seen a real one. They had people there day and night typing in commands and codes that somehow kept track of their cargo. They tried to train me how to do it and were very patient even though I had no idea what was going on. After three days, however, I finally said, *this is ridiculous*, and I quit.

I was out of work for a while after that and things started to look pretty bleak. I didn't know what I was going to do until my old boss at Sky Chefs called two weeks later and said they had an opening that I might be interested in. The position entailed supervising the wait staff at their restaurants in the TWA Building at JFK. The hours were seven in the morning to three in the afternoon, Sunday through Thursday, and I could start immediately. After my last couple of jobs I wasn't exactly optimistic about this one, especially since I had zero experience supervising employees and had never been a waitress myself. At that point, I had no other prospects and decided to give it a try.

As it turned out, I loved the job. The management staff was young and I had actually given some of them their tours of the facilities when I was working for Sky Chefs in Manhattan. The wait staff all had been doing their job for some time at this location so they did not require any training from me. My office duties included the daily sales report and the handling of the cash flow. The job was only twenty minutes from my home and I could drive to it. I did not miss the Long Island Rail Road! The hours were still long, five days a week, but the days went by quickly because I wasn't cooped up in an office all day and was usually running to and from the different restaurants in the building. It was really a lot of fun and I was relieved that I had finally found a job that I liked, but then in October I received a letter from Dallas.

I was informed that American was resuming flight attendant training and that I had been enrolled in the November 11 class. They had apparently saved my spot in the class even after I left the company.

Since I was back working for Sky Chefs, all I had to do was report to the flight academy in Dallas for training.

When Doug got home from work I showed him the letter.

"This is great!" he said excitedly after reading it.

"I don't know if I want to go," I said.

"What?" he asked incredulously. "Why not?"

"Well, I'm married now, I really like the job that I have, and I just don't know anymore if I really want to do this."

"Oh no," he said. "You're doing this. You've wanted to do this your whole life. I don't want you turning forty with kids running around and saying, *Oh, I could have been a flight attendant*, but because you married me you didn't do it. Even if you go to training and then fly only one trip and quit, that would be fine, but you have to go. I don't want you to have any regrets! This is your dream come true!" My husband is a very wise man because I would have thrown it back in his face long before I turned forty!

3.

Six Weeks in Dallas

I cried all the way to the airport. Doug kept telling me that I would be fine. He said that he'd miss me and that he'd call whenever he could. He assured me that before I knew it the six weeks would be over. I still didn't want to go. This was partly due to the fact that becoming a flight attendant had been a companion of mine since I was seven years old. Now I was worried that the reality might not turn out to be as good as the dream. Most of it, however, had to do with not wanting to leave Doug for so long. We had only been married six months. Now we were about to say good-bye for six weeks. *Six whole weeks!* It sounded like an eternity.

When we got to LaGuardia, Doug parked in the short-term lot and accompanied me into the terminal. Back then you didn't need a boarding pass to get through security, so he held my hand all the way to the gate. I cried the whole time and people were staring, but I didn't care. All I knew was that I didn't want to leave him.

While we were waiting for the flight to start boarding, I recognized a young woman whom I had seen when I went to the interview in Dallas; which at this point was about a year earlier. I stopped crying long enough to ask her if she was going down for training, and she said she was. She was talking to a few other people who were also going and they introduced themselves. Instead of staying and talking to them, I went back to Doug. I wanted to be with him every last possible second before stepping on that plane.

The trainees had all been assigned seats in the same row on the flight. When our row was announced for boarding, the others all looked over at me to see if I was coming. I pretended not to notice. None of them said anything because they probably thought that I just needed a little extra time to say good-bye to my husband. They didn't realize that I needed a lot more time because I stayed with him until the rest of the passengers were on the plane and the final boarding call was made. Doug and I were the only two people left at the gate. As the agent was making the announcement over the P.A. system, she was looking right at us as if talking directly to me. Doug kept telling me that I had to go, but I wouldn't let go.

Finally, after they had given up on me and closed the aircraft door, I decided to get on the plane. The agent looked at me like I was crazy when I told her that I had to get on that flight. They decided to let me on anyway and opened the door again. I kissed Doug good-bye one last time and hurried onto the plane. By the time I changed my mind again not to go, it was already too late because we were taxiing down the runway.

An hour into the flight, I still hadn't stopped crying. The other trainees were sitting across the aisle from me talking amongst themselves and not really acknowledging me. Probably because they thought I was nuts! At one point one of the flight attendants working the flight came over to say hello to them because she had heard that they were on their way to training. She started telling them what to expect and how much fun they were going to have and so forth. The girl sitting across the aisle from me interrupted her and mentioned that I was going too.

The flight attendant turned and looked at me incredulously.

"*You?*" she said. "You have got to be kidding me! You haven't stopped crying since you boarded this plane! You'll never make it!"

"Yes I will," I said, more to myself than to her, and suddenly I felt different about the whole thing. Maybe I needed someone to challenge me like that because when we got to Dallas, her words kept echoing through my mind and I started getting mad. *Who was she to say that I'll never make it?* Although I did not know this person and there was a very good possibility that I would never see her again, I wanted to prove her wrong. So, instead of jumping on the first flight back to New York like I had been thinking about doing since taxiing down the runway at LaGuardia, I went with the others to check in at the flight services office.

We were informed upon our arrival that the dormitories at the flight academy were filled to capacity, so for the first two weeks we would have to stay at a hotel and be shuttled to and from campus. This did not sound like a fun time. It was, however, a good opportunity to get used to staying in hotels and taking shuttles since that is what we would be doing on layovers when we became flight attendants. It also seemed like it might be a little easier to get used to being away from home in a hotel room rather than a dorm since I had stayed at hotels before but had never been in a dorm.

As soon as we checked in, I went right up to my room and called Doug to let him know where I was. He told me to hang up and that he would call right back so I wouldn't be charged for making long distance calls. When he called back, we talked for a long time and he managed to calm my nerves somewhat. Eventually he said that he had to go because if we talked this long every night for the next six weeks, he was going to have to find a second job just to pay the phone bill.

Each of us was assigned roommates. Since it was Saturday night, my roommate decided to go out to the bars with some of the other trainees. I had been invited along too, but I politely declined because I didn't think going out to bars was something that married women should do. So I stayed in the room by myself and watched TV while fighting the urge to call Doug again.

The next morning, I had breakfast downstairs at the restaurant with some of the other trainees; most of whom had already gotten to know each other a little the night before, but hadn't met me yet. They had made plans to go to Six Flags Over Texas, an amusement park, after breakfast and invited me to come along. I accepted.

About twenty of us went to the park. I was a little uncomfortable at first because everybody was talking like they had known each other for years and I felt like an outsider. Also, they all seemed to be single, which made them seem younger than me even though just about everyone was my age or older (I would later find out that out of sixty people in the training class, I was only one of three who was married). But everyone was really nice and I made a lot of new friends. By the end of the day, we had formed a bond with each other since we were all far from our homes and that for the next six weeks we were in this thing together. I was also relieved to hear that just about everyone was nervous about starting classes the next morning. After seeing how calm and collected the trainees I flew down with from New York seemed to be, I had been worried that I was going to be the only nervous wreck.

Although flight attendant training was often referred to as "Barbie Boot Camp" or the "Charm Farm," it was actually pretty intense and a lot of hard work. Appearance was important. We had lessons on hair regulations, makeup, how to walk, speak properly, and how to greet passengers with a warm, friendly smile! That was just the beginning of it. Most of the time, we were sitting in classrooms learning emergency medical procedures. This included C.P.R. and first-aid. We were taught what to do during a loss of cabin pressurization, how to deal with unruly passengers, and procedures for just about every other in-flight emergency situation. We had to memorize aircraft diagrams. We had to learn how to recognize fire hazards. We had to learn how to prepare the cabin in the event of a crash landing and we had to participate in evacuation drills in the simulator building where they had simulators for every aircraft that American flew. We were also taught how to inflate the slides that are stored next to each exit and how to use them to evacuate passengers and ourselves from the plane. This was pretty scary at first because it was a very steep drop of approximately thirty feet and we all had to take the plunge. The simulator building also had a big pool for learning the ditching procedures in the event of a water landing. There were drills where we jumped off the wing into the water and then climbed into the evacuation slide, which was also used as a raft. Everything was timed and everything had to be done in order and exactly correct. It was exciting, but it was also a little intimidating. There were so many things to remember and they had to be done quickly and precisely.

Throughout training, it felt like you were under a microscope. Out of the sixty people in the class, approximately forty graduated. At any time they could ask you to leave for any reason—if you failed a test, if you showed up late to class, or if you just weren't what American wanted as an employee! If you were asked to leave, you were told just prior to entering the classroom in the morning and escorted back to your room to pack your things and clear out before your roommates returned. An empty seat in the classroom was a pretty good indication that the person who was supposed to be sitting there had been asked to leave. The remaining trainees were never informed why someone had been asked to leave. Afterwards, there were always a lot of rumors and speculation as to the reason. It seemed like kind of a cold way to handle it, but I guess they didn't want to bring down the morale of everyone who was still there by having to say emotional good-byes or hearing the person who was kicked out say bad things about the experience. It also kept us on our toes because we knew that if we weren't careful, any one of us could be next.

Having to stay at a hotel those first two weeks did turn out to be a disappointment, not only because we had to take the shuttles to and from campus, but also because we felt so isolated from the rest of the academy when we weren't there. We made the best of it, however, by having nightly group study sessions in one of our rooms for a couple of hours to prepare for the next day's test (of which there was one every day in class). Afterwards we would hang out or watch TV until it was time to go to sleep.

One night while a group of us were hanging out, the subject of chugging beer came up. When I mentioned that I was a good chugger, nobody believed me. Since I hadn't gone out that first night or the following weekend and had been kind of quiet and shy so far, I must not have seemed to them like the chugging type.

"*You?*" my friend Peter said incredulously. "You don't even drink!"

"I'm actually a pretty good chugger," I said.

"Oh yeah? Then put up your ten bucks—we'll have a chugging contest!"

I'm a German girl, so when it comes to chugging beer, I can hold my own. Needless to say, it didn't surprise me in the least when I won the contest, but everyone else was shocked, especially Peter.

Peter is still a good friend of mine, and even after all these years he still brings it up. Whenever I see him he says, "I still can't believe you beat me in that chugging contest!" He is a great guy, and his encouragement was one of the main reasons I made it through training. Whenever he found me in tears just after I had talked to Doug on the phone, he would say, "Come on, Keiser—were you talking to your husband again? Stop crying, we only have five more weeks left—you can do this!" The next week it would be, "We only have four more weeks left" or three weeks and so on. He had a knack for offering encouragement when I needed it the most, and sometimes I wonder if I would have graduated without him.

After my hijacking ten years, later he said to me, "I feel bad now because if I hadn't always encouraged you to stay, you would have never been in that position."

"Peter," I said, "The only person I hold accountable for that night was that crazy man who was pointing a gun at my head. You shouldn't feel responsible for that. Besides, I still love being a flight attendant— that's what you should feel responsible for!"

After two weeks at the hotel, we finally got to move into the dorms, which was much better. Now we could just walk to class instead of taking the shuttles. The campus was beautiful and looked like a real university, so I did get a little taste of college life after all. My two years at Nassau Community didn't really feel like college because I just drove there to go to class and then drove right back home. I never spent any more time there than I had to. Ironically, the Nassau Community campus resembled more of what I thought a flight academy would look like because it was built on an old airfield and some of the buildings were actually old airplane hangars.

One of the drawbacks of living in the dorms, however, was that we didn't have phones in our suites like we did in the hotel rooms. There was a pay phone out in the hallway, so Doug and I had to set up times when he would call. This was alright if I happened to be in the suite, but if I was out somewhere I would have to hurry back to the dorm so I wouldn't miss his call. It was too expensive to call him collect, and I usually didn't have enough spare change to keep plugging coins into the phone every few minutes because our conversations typically lasted a while.

I didn't miss a single one of Doug's calls until one Friday evening when I finally broke down and went out to a Country & Western bar with some of my classmates. I knew I was going to miss his call, but I was tired of sitting around doing nothing on Friday and Saturday nights after a tough week of training. I decided to join my new friends for a few drinks. After all, I was in love and happily married-not in prison! I went out and had a really good time. When I got in at around two in the morning, there were several messages on the bulletin board next to the pay phone saying that Doug had called. The first one said that at 8:00 PM he had called, and the one suitemate of mine who stayed in that night took it upon herself to tell him that I had been out Christmas shopping, which was believable since it was early December. The next message was from 10:00 PM, and she wrote that she had told him that the stores in Dallas were open late during the holiday season. There was one from 11:00 PM and then another from midnight, and that one said, *Alright, Doug doesn't believe the stores are open this late—you'd better call him as soon as you get in!* I called him and he could tell I was a little tipsy. He was glad to hear that I had a good time, especially since the last time he had seen me I was crying my eyes out and saying that I didn't want to go to training. After that night, I became part of the group that went out on the weekends and no longer felt guilty about it. I'm sure Doug was joining his friends on those weekends also.

It took a few weeks to finally let go of the glamorous flight attendant fantasy that had been with me since I was seven, but once I did adjust to the rigorous training and accept that I was going to have to work hard in order to graduate, I started to enjoy it. I was glad that this job wasn't just about looking pretty and serving drinks to passengers and that flight attendants really are an essential part of the flight crew.

Even so, in those days looking pretty was still part of the job, particularly when it came to the strict weight requirements. We were weighed every Monday morning, and the maximum weight was ridiculously low. If you were even an ounce over the limit for your height, they would send you home. One Sunday morning, I stepped on the scale and discovered that I was two pounds over and went into a panic because I had no idea how I was going to lose that much weight in twenty-four hours. I exercised all day and evening and didn't eat a thing. When I weighed myself before bed I was still a pound over. Finally one of my suitemates suggested taking a laxative.

I took the laxative before bed and it didn't kick in until the next morning about a half-hour before class. Everyone thought it was just the funniest thing in the world and they were all cracking jokes. I was really nervous because now not only was I overweight, I was also going to be late for class. Tardiness was a very serious offense in training since being on time is extremely important in the airline industry, but at the moment I had no choice.

Fortunately my suitemates covered for me and said that I was really sick and throwing up. I finally showed up forty-five minutes late. After what I had just been through I must have really looked sick because none of the instructors even questioned me. When I stepped on the scale I was afraid to look. I came in a full pound under and got to stay! That was a little too close for comfort, however, and afterwards I was much more cautious and started weighing myself every day so I wouldn't have to go through that again.

Today, management isn't allowed to mention your weight unless you can't fit into the jump seat harness. That would be a safety issue since it would inhibit you from doing your job properly. Back when I first started, however, we got weighed once a year during our annual physicals. If you were overweight you had to shed those extra pounds in a matter of days or else you could be suspended or even fired. Even if you just looked a little overweight, a supervisor could pull you aside and order you to step on a scale. I could only imagine how quickly a lawsuit would be filed if somebody tried that today!

cᴧɔ

During the second half of training, our weekends were spent doing "observation rides" to see how the working flight attendants did their jobs. Then we did "work flights," which meant that you worked a real flight as an extra flight attendant but were not considered part of the main crew since you still weren't F.A.A. certified. This was very exciting because you were really doing the job except that you sat in a passenger seat rather than the jump seats where the flight attendants normally sat.

For your first observation ride, you got to pick where to go as long as it was a "narrow-bodied aircraft," which is a plane that has a single aisle between seats. There was no question where I wanted to go, so I called Doug to meet me at LaGuardia and to bring some of the things that I had forgotten to take with me to Dallas.

The flight went well, but I probably didn't do as much observing as I should have because I was too busy thinking about seeing Doug. At LaGuardia he was waiting for me at the gate and I ran into his arms. We had barely said hello when he said, "Come on, we're leaving."

"What do you mean we're leaving?" I said. "I only have two hours before my flight back!"

"Don't worry; you'll be back in time."

"Well, where are we going?"

Unbeknownst to me, Doug had booked a room at one of the hotels across the street from the airport. Being young newlyweds, I don't think I have to fill in the details. When we got back to the airport a short time later, my classmates who had also chosen New York for their observation rides knew exactly what we had done and gave us a round of applause. I was *so* embarrassed—no, I was *mortified*. They teased me all the way back to Texas. I'm sure they wished they had someone waiting for them instead of having to sit in the terminal for two hours!

One of the most exciting days of training is when the home bases are assigned to the trainees. For me it was one of the most nerve-wracking because not everyone gets their first choice. That might have been okay for some of the others who weren't married, but I had a husband in New York and I didn't want to be anywhere else. In the end I got assigned to New York. This was a huge relief because I might have quit had I been assigned elsewhere!

After the bases were assigned, the managers of some of the new apartment buildings in New York sent representatives down to Dallas to try and get the New York based flight attendants to rent in their buildings. Rupert Towers on 90th Street was one of them and they were just opening up. They made some nice deals for flight attendants and offered limo rides to the airport for early morning flights. The rent was pretty affordable at the time, so quite a few of them picked out roommates and signed a lease.

Living with a group of girls in the city sounded like a lot of fun, but I already had a roommate at home. After listening to the others pick out roommates and talk about how much fun they were going to have, I did start to get a little jealous. But I knew that I already had something they were eventually going to want, perhaps sooner than they realized—a good husband—so I was able to get over it rather easily. And though I don't have any regrets, I do still occasionally wonder what it would have been like to live the flight attendant lifestyle as a single girl for a while.

As upset as I was on the way down to Dallas to begin training, I turned out to be one of the few people who actually enjoyed the experience and was sad when it was over. In six weeks, I had gone from one extreme to the other and didn't know if I really wanted to go home, especially since I wasn't sure if I was ready to start doing this job for real.

Graduation day was very emotional because I knew that afterwards I wasn't going to see many of my fellow trainees who had been assigned to other bases for a long time, if ever again. There was a big ceremony in which we got our flight wings pinned to our uniforms and a brief reception afterwards, and then we were taken to the airport to fly to our assigned home bases.

Most New York-based domestic flight attendants were based out of LaGuardia, and since you had to have six months on the job before you were eligible to work international flights, that's where all the trainees who were assigned to New York wound up. When we arrived from Dallas, we were greeted at the gate by flight service representatives and escorted down to the crew scheduling office. We had to fill out some paperwork and then we were given our first month schedules. When the man who had processed my paperwork handed me my schedule, I just stared at it thinking there was a misprint or something because it didn't seem to make any sense. My first day of flight duty went something like this:

New York-Chicago
Chicago-Detroit
Detroit-Washington
Washington-New York

"Oh my goodness!" I said after finally realizing what it meant. "I thought you only did one flight per day!"

He looked at me like I had two heads and then turned to one of his colleagues.

"We've got a live one here!" he said loudly enough for everyone in the room to hear. A few people laughed, but I was about ready to start crying because nobody ever said anything to me about having to work four flights in one day!

4.

Rookie

As if I wasn't nervous enough the night before my first trip, crew scheduling had assigned me into the number one position; I was going to be the lead flight attendant of an experienced crew despite having no experience myself. Yet, this was only the least of my concerns. While I wanted to earn the respect of my fellow crew members and show them that I knew what I was doing, I was more worried about making mistakes and embarrassing myself in front of the passengers and having them turn against me like a pack of hungry wolves. At the very least, I thought the crew would be on my side; that they would be understanding and nice like my classmates in training and help me out if I got in trouble. Little did I know that they were the ones I should have been worried about!

That first trip consisted of three legs over two days: New York to Detroit, Detroit to Toronto with a one night layover in Toronto, and Toronto to New York the following day. Things started out relatively smoothly on the first flight. I greeted the passengers, made the announcements, and I managed to make it through my checklist of pre-flight procedures without an incident. Up in the air, I was assigned to work the first class section by myself, and that didn't seem so bad either. I served the passengers their drinks, gave them their hot towels, took their meal orders and handed them out without managing to spill anything on anyone! I did it all without receiving a single complaint! At one point I stood up front with arms folded satisfactorily and watched everyone contentedly eating their meals wishing that my instructors from the flight academy were there to see how well I was doing.

Somewhere over Lake Erie, the captain made an announcement that we would be landing in Detroit in approximately thirty minutes. After the announcement, one of the other flight attendants came up front and asked me if I needed any help.

"No," I said confidently. "I think I've got everything under control."

"So, you're all done?" she asked skeptically. "All the trays are picked up and put away?"

"No," I said. "They're still eating."

"What do you mean they're still eating? We're landing in half-hour! You should have had everything put away by now!"

"You mean we're not supposed to wait until they're finished?"

"No! For heaven's sake, are you stupid or something? You have to get this stuff put away now! Don't they teach you people anything down at the charm farm?"

I was ready to start crying on the spot, but I managed to hold back my tears while the two of us hastily collected the trays and put everything away. My voice was a little shaky when I made the final announcements and I thought I was going to burst into tears while the passengers were deplaning, but I managed to keep my smile just wide enough to hide how upset I was.

As soon as I completed all my post-flight duties, I hurried into the terminal and called Doug.

"They're so mean!" I cried into the phone, letting it all out. "This one flight attendant got mad at me and asked if I was stupid!"

As soon as I had said this, I noticed the very flight attendant I was talking about heading in my direction.

"Wait a minute, she's coming!" I said and hung up on Doug. I didn't want her to see that I had been crying, so I subtly wiped the tears from my cheeks and turned in the direction she was coming from. I casually walked away from the phone right towards her and gave her the best smile I could muster up, but she returned it with a glare and continued on her way. After she disappeared from view, I found another phone in a more discreet location and called Doug back and started crying some more. He was able to calm me down enough to convince me to get back on the plane and work the next leg of the trip.

The flight to Toronto went a little more smoothly since it was a much shorter flight and there wasn't a meal service. After we landed and all the passengers had deplaned, I took a deep breath of relief that I had survived my first day on the job. On the shuttle to the hotel, the flight attendant who had gotten mad at me earlier softened up a little and asked me if I wanted to join the rest of the crew for dinner. Although none of the other crew members had been very nice to me either and were barely acknowledging my presence, I accepted the invitation. It seemed like a better alternative than sitting in the hotel room by myself and crying.

While we were at dinner, I noticed that I wasn't the only one being ignored. It turned out that the woman who had gotten mad at me was also a fairly new flight attendant, and the other, more experienced crew members were ignoring her too. She was the only one who was even willing to talk to me, and later when the others weren't around, she apologized and explained that she had been upset because they were being rude to her and she in turn unfairly took it out on me. She told me that flight attendants were a cliquey bunch and that the cliques were pretty much determined by how much experience you had.

"Don't take it personally," she said. "I found out the hard way that a lot of them don't like working with new people because they think it's going to make their jobs more difficult and some of them are just snobs. Just keep in mind that it's them, not you. And if they're giving you a hard time and it starts getting to you, just remind yourself that on the next trip you'll be working with a different crew."

Despite our rocky start, we became good friends over the years and even socialized outside of work together with our husbands. Her advice proved invaluable to me in my career. Whether it was a passenger giving me a hard time or a fellow crew member, once I learned how not to take it personally, the job became much easier. Of course, it's very difficult not to take it personally when somebody treats you like yesterday's trash, but after a while you realize that some people are going to be rude no matter how nice you are or how well you do your job. When you do come across someone like that, all you can do is back off and let them be. You are only going to drive yourself crazy if you try to please them.

Every crew is different, and the crew you wind up with is usually the biggest factor on how well a trip goes. Before the era of computers, you were not able to check who the other crewmembers assigned to your trip would be. You never knew who you would be working with until you signed in for your trip at the airport. If you were lucky enough to wind up with a crew in which everyone was nice, the job was a blast and you loved every minute of it. If the trip involved a layover, you got to go out to dinner and sightsee-it was like a mini-vacation with your friends. If you wound up with a bad crew, the best thing to do was just focus on your own job and not worry about what everyone else was doing and keep reminding yourself that you won't be working with these people again on the next trip. Quite often, the crews were a mixture of good and bad, and in those instances it was easy to make a lot of friends with the nice flight attendants since you had the common bond of having to endure working a trip together with some who weren't so nice.

Overall, I enjoyed working with all these different people and personalities and was glad that I wasn't stuck in an office working with the same people every day. I also liked that the job wasn't just a dull routine where you couldn't tell one day from the next, and working with different people all the time made it much easier to remember each particular trip. After a while, even some of the people who weren't so nice at first became a bit more congenial once I became confident that I knew what I was doing. But getting to that point took a little while...

One of the questions they ask during your first interview is, "Why do you want to become a flight attendant?" I don't think there is a flight attendant working today, myself included, who didn't say something like, "I love to travel and I love people." Well, that goes to show you how naive most of us were about what we were getting ourselves into!

My second trip started with an early morning New York to Chicago flight that had a 5:00 AM sign-in and a 6:00 AM departure. This meant that I had to get up at three in the morning, which was an especially difficult task for me because I'm not a morning person. I was dead tired and all the passengers on that plane that morning seemed to be also. They were businessmen who had their heads buried in *The New York Times* or *The Wall Street Journal*, or they were just talking to each other about business. They couldn't care less about telling the flight attendants about the exciting adventures that awaited them in Chicago!

This was about a two hour flight and we served a full breakfast. At that time, we didn't have carts so we had to run the meals out and then run the dirty trays back in. After the passengers had finished eating, you would load up with as many of the dirty trays as you could carry and bring them back to the galley and stick them into the carriers, which are removable compartments that are taken off the plane later for cleaning.

After one of my runs, I was in the galley stuffing dirty trays into one of the carriers while one of the other flight attendants was behind me loading trays into the opposite carrier. With the two of us, there was very little room to maneuver back there. At one point, I dropped a piece of silverware on the floor and had to crouch awkwardly to pick it up. As I was doing so, I bumped into the stack of trays that I hadn't yet loaded and spilled a half-filled cup of coffee that was on the top tray down my face and all over my blouse.

Oh yeah, this is glamorous, I said to myself while hastily trying to get myself cleaned up. As I was doing so, I thought about that woman from training with the heavy Texas accent who taught us grooming and how important our appearance was with regards to everything we did. One day, she commented that my walk was a horror show because it was way too fast. I remember being really annoyed at that and thinking, *Well, I'm a New Yorker, honey, and we don't do anything slow!* Now her words annoyed me even more because everything about this job involved doing things quickly or else they would never get done on time. I really would have liked her to tell me that I was moving too fast now!

When I resumed loading the dirty trays into the other carrier, the flight attendant who had been working behind me was in the cabin gathering more trays, so for the moment I was back there by myself. I took advantage of the extra space by crouching down a little more while I was loading my trays, which was slightly more comfortable and made it less likely that I would spill anything on myself again. After I finished loading my trays, I stood up and the back of my pants got caught on the handle of the carrier door behind me. I heard the distinct sound of fabric being torn. It happened so quickly that I didn't know what it was at first until I turned around and saw the damage.

"Oh no!" I said and suddenly went into a panic.

The entire left cheek had ripped out from the seat of my pants, leaving nothing to the imagination as to what I was wearing underneath. To make matters worse, I had only had these pants for two weeks and they weren't even paid for yet. These weren't the cheap polyester uniforms we have today that start to shred after you wash them too many times- these were nice, red, expensive Bill Blass designer pants. As if that wasn't enough, this was only the first leg of a three day trip and these were the only uniform pants I had, so I didn't know what I was going to do.

For the time being I tied the strings of my topper, which is basically an apron, around my rear to hold the torn flap on the seat of my pants in place and cover the exposed area. After landing in Chicago I left the topper on, which is okay to wear when you're up in the air doing the dirty work, but in the terminal it was considered a major flight attendant fashion faux pas. Sure enough, an airline supervisor spotted me and started screaming at me about wearing a topper in the terminal. On the verge of tears I explained to her how my pants were ripped and I didn't know what to do, so she sent me to flight services because they had spare uniform pieces down there. Unfortunately, they did not have my size, so for the next couple of days I had to squeeze my size four butt into a size two pair of pants, which was not very comfortable and far from being glamorous. But, taking the advice of that woman in Dallas, I walked very slowly and carefully and managed to make it back to New York without splitting them.

During my second month, I had my first experience being on reserve, which most flight attendants will tell you is one of their least favorite aspects of the job. Being on reserve meant that you did not have any scheduled trips for that particular month. You had to be on call all month and ready to take any trip assigned to you with a two hour report time to any of the three major airports in the New York metropolitan area-Kennedy, LaGuardia, or Newark. When I first started, we were required to be on reserve every other month. This was particularly difficult since this was a time when cell phones did not exist. You couldn't leave the house without first calling for permission from crew schedule. Answering machines and cordless phones weren't common household items yet either, and since all we had was an old-fashioned phone that plugged into a jack on the wall, I was almost afraid to go to the bathroom or take a shower at first because I was too worried about missing a call. You couldn't make plans to do anything, you couldn't go anywhere-you basically had no social life. All you did was sit around for that month watching TV and waiting for the phone to ring. It was like being under house arrest!

When you did get called out for trips while you were on reserve, they were usually very inconvenient. One time you'd get a night trip and then the next one would be an early morning trip. You had to learn to function with sleep deprivation. Not only that, you were usually just an "extra" flight attendant on these trips, and extras didn't always stay with the crew. If you got assigned to a trip to L.A. with a stopover in Phoenix, you would often work just the first leg out to Phoenix and have to stay there by yourself while the rest of the crew continued on to L.A., which was difficult for me because I didn't like to be stranded in strange cities by myself. Because you were only "the extra," the crew didn't really consider you one of them and often didn't bother to even ask your name. They hardly even acknowledged you except when they said, "Go do this" or "Go do that."

Being on reserve isn't good for your figure either! When you're trapped in the house all day, there's not much else to do besides sitting in front of the TV and eating. When teenagers go away to college, they often put on the "freshman fifteen," but being on reserve can easily lead to the "flight attendant fifteen." And when you were called out on a trip, there was usually a layover involved, which meant going out to eat for several meals in a row. If I was by myself it was easier to watch what I ate, but if I had a layover with a crew and we all went out to eat together, it was difficult to resist temptation. This was especially true with more experienced crews because they knew where all the good restaurants were to sample the local flavor. The first time I was in Phoenix with a crew I mentioned that I had never eaten Mexican food. Naturally, we went out to a Mexican Restaurant and the cockpit crew did all the ordering and I tried everything. Over a short period of time I got to sample what kind of food many of the states were famous for, and in the process I put on a few pounds that I would pay for later with diet and exercise. It was worth it because I got a taste of what life was like in different regions of the country and got to see how much different people were outside of New York, which is one of the aspects of the job that appealed to me in the first place.

Even after I settled into the job and learned how to adjust to the many different personalities I wound up working with, nothing could have prepared me for one particular three day trip during my first summer on the job. The trip was scheduled for layovers in Detroit and L.A. The trip started out okay and the first day of flying went fine even though I was not looking forward to spending the night in Ann Arbor, Michigan, the Detroit layover city.

I had never been to Ann Arbor and didn't think there would be anything to see or do there like there would be in a more exotic city such as L.A. or San Francisco, but it actually turned out to be one of my favorite domestic layover stops. It was a big college town and there were always festivals going on and all these great restaurants and so forth, and the people there were a lot friendlier there than they usually were in the big cities.

That first time I was there, the captain we were flying with suggested that we eat at a restaurant called The Whiffle Tree. I had never flown with this captain before and he seemed very strict and did everything by the book down to the letter, but he still acted like an okay guy at first. When we sat down to dinner, I ordered trout and was expecting it to be served as a filet. I was somewhat taken aback when it was served completely in tact—fins, gills and an eye that was facing up and staring right at me. Everyone else started eating, but I just sat there trying not to look down at my plate.

"Is there a problem with your food?" the captain asked with a tone that hinted he was a little offended that I wasn't enjoying my meal at the restaurant he had selected.

"Yes," I said. "I can't eat something that's staring at me."

"Waitress!" he said so suddenly and loudly that most of us jumped in our seats. I don't know if it was just the way he said it or if this waitress had served him before, but she was at the table in an instant. "The lady sitting right there would appreciate it if you took her trout back and severed the head."

"Yes, sir," the waitress said and took my plate back into the kitchen. A minute later she returned with the decapitated fish, and I instantly lost the rest of what little appetite I had left, but I did my best to eat it. The captain kept looking at me to make sure that I was. I felt like a child who had been ordered by her parents to eat her vegetables or else go right up to bed without dessert.

The next morning all of the flight attendants and cockpit crew got up a little early and had breakfast without the captain down at the hotel restaurant. The rest of the flight crew was really nice and it was a much more relaxed atmosphere than it had been at dinner the night before. We had a shuttle van scheduled for a 7:00 AM pickup, but at around 6:45 the captain stormed into the restaurant and started yelling at us.

"Does anybody plan on working today?" he said. "The van is out there waiting! Come on, let's go!"

We wolfed down our coffee and paid the bill only to rush outside and find that the van wasn't there. To put it mildly, we were all a bit peeved, but we couldn't say anything because he was, after all, the captain. The van arrived ten minutes later at exactly 7:00 a.m. We all piled in and nobody said a word all the way to the airport because we already knew that it was going to be a long, long day working our way out to L.A. with this guy at the helm and two stops in between. When we finally did get to L.A. that evening, the captain's wife met him at the gate and she rode in the shuttle van with us to the hotel.

Back then, flight attendants had to share hotel rooms during layovers, and that night I wound up in the bed that was closest to the door that adjoined our room to the one next door. Since we didn't have reservations for an adjoining room and didn't know who was staying next door, I just assumed that the door would be locked. The flight attendant I was rooming with asked me to check just to make sure. I reluctantly got out of bed and turned the knob fully expecting it to be locked, but to my surprise the door opened and I saw a man and a woman in the room next door making love. I quickly closed the door and locked it. In disbelief, I turned to my roommate and told her what I had just seen. Moments later, the man from next door started pounding on the door and yelling like a maniac for us to open up. We didn't know what to do but opening that door was not an option! I didn't know what he was so mad about because I had only seen what was happening for a split second, but he was yelling through the door with murderous rage and we thought he truly wanted to kill us.

"Do you think it was the captain?" my roommate asked.

"No," I said, not thinking that someone with such an esteemed position as a captain for a major commercial airline was capable of such behavior. "Actually, I couldn't tell, but I don't think the captain would act this crazy."

"Well, you saw how he behaved this morning, and it actually does kind of sound like him a little."

"Maybe we can find out."

While the crazy man continued to yell and pound on the door, I called the front desk and asked what room the captain was staying in. Nowadays, hotels won't tell you what room number someone is in but will let you call the room, but back then at this particular hotel, they didn't have such a policy and the person at the front desk did indeed confirm that the captain was in the room right next door.

I was mortified that it was our captain but also thought it a little funny!

The pounding went on for most of the night and the two of us sat up terrified that he was eventually going to break the door down. Never in my life have I heard someone as angry as this man was. We didn't want to call security because we thought we might get in trouble for opening the door in the first place, but we were even more worried about the captain knowing that it was us. I don't know why his wife didn't try to do anything to stop him, but she may have been just as afraid of him as we were, maybe even more so. After several hours, he finally gave up and all was quiet again, but we were still too scared to get any sleep.

The next morning, the entire crew was outside waiting for the shuttle van to the airport. We were out there a few minutes early, but the captain was nowhere to be found. After the shuttle arrived and we all climbed in, we waited several minutes past the scheduled departure time, but there was still no sign of the captain.

"Alright, let's go," the first officer said to the driver and then turned to us. "I don't feel bad at all about leaving him behind after the way he treated us yesterday!"

About halfway to the airport the shuttle dispatcher got on the radio and said to the driver, "We have the captain here and he wants to know who gave the authorization to leave without him." Nobody said anything, and after a long, uncomfortable silence, the dispatcher finally just told the driver to turn around and come back to pick up the captain.

By now my roommate and I were so terrified of this man that we hadn't even told the rest of the crew about the night before, so they were a little more startled than we were when he stormed up to the shuttle and started screaming at us.

"Who told the van driver to leave?" His face was crimson and bits of spittle were shooting out of his mouth as he screamed. "Which one of you gave authorization for this shuttle to proceed to the airport?" He looked us over with wild eyes, and of course nobody admitted it because he looked like he wanted to kill someone.

"I'm having a really bad day so far!" he continued, suddenly calmer but still with a raised voice. "I got almost no sleep last night, and on top of that an intruder burst into my room in the middle of the night!"

He left out the part that he was making love to his wife at the time and that he spent half the night banging on the door afterwards, but fortunately he did not seem to know that it was one of us who had interrupted him. The thought had crossed our minds that he could have just as easily called the front desk like we did and asked what room each of us were staying in. Apparently, it had not occurred to him to do so! At this point I couldn't even look at my roommate-not because I was afraid I was going to start laughing, but I just didn't want to give the captain the slightest hint that it had been one of us. Who knows what this maniac would have done if he knew, and in a couple of hours he was going to fly us all the way back to New York!

It wasn't long after this trip that I became eligible to work international flights and decided to give it a try. For one thing, I was tired of flying with the often unfriendly domestic crews, and I was also tired of working thirteen, fourteen hour days going up and down, up and down. I sometimes worked five or six flights in one day and never got past Boston or Toronto. It was exhausting having to run through all the procedures over and over again, serving the beverages and snacks and then ten minutes later having to collect all the trash and prepare the cabin for landing only to do it all over again an hour later. No wonder domestic crews were so grouchy! International flights were generally longer and you normally wouldn't do more than one or two a day. You could take your time doing the meal service and cleaning up, which made it seem like it would be much less hectic. I couldn't imagine continuing to work the domestic flights for any extended amount of time because I was already frazzled from doing it for six months. If international wasn't any better, I would just have to accept that I had given the flight attendant career an honest try and then try to find something else to do for the rest of my life.

After I was accepted to international, I had to go back down to Dallas for an additional week of over-water training. We did a lot of ditching drills, raft procedures, studied the aircrafts used for international flights, and so on. When the week was up, I was assigned to JFK as my home base. Upon landing back in New York, I felt like I had arrived at a moment of truth at the very place where it had all begun sixteen years earlier.

As it turned out, international flying was a completely different world and I absolutely loved it. At the time, American had just purchased Trans-Caribbean Airlines, so I usually worked flights down to the Caribbean with mixed crews of American flight attendants based at JFK and Trans-Caribbean flight attendants based in San Juan. We mostly flew turnarounds from JFK, which was nice because it was usually just one flight there and one flight back with very few layovers. The crews were much nicer and much more relaxed than the domestic crews. There was a comradariere amongst the crewmembers and I found my niche among them. At that time, many of the international flights were on 747s, which was a fun plane to work in. It not only had an upper deck, but it also had two lower lobe galleys if you needed to get away from the passengers for a few minutes or to chit-chat with your fellow crewmembers. Suddenly everything I had been through to get to that point made it seem all worthwhile. Looking back now, I know that I truly loved it or else I wouldn't have continued doing it for the next thirty years!

Despite having finally gotten to where I wanted to be with my career, flying did become a little bit of a strain on my marriage. I was constantly away from home and often had to work weekends and holidays while Doug worked the more conventional Monday-through-

Friday/nine-to-five schedule down on Wall Street. We didn't get to spend as much time together as we would have liked. He was understanding about it, however, because he knew how much being a flight attendant meant to me. We really made an effort to make it work. He would often accompany me on weekend trips when I had a layover or took a day off here and there to fly somewhere with me. We got to see a good part of the world together over all these years. It was like one long honeymoon with a lot of breaks in between!

The one thing, however, that I could not stand about this job was being on reserve. Every other month for three years, I had to sit at home unable to commit to weddings or social events or anything because I never knew when they were going to call and tell me to go somewhere. Finally, after three years I had accumulated enough seniority to be on reserve only every fourth month, but even that was difficult when I had Kirsten and Kelly. If it hadn't been for my parents living nearby to baby-sit, I probably would have had to quit. They were great about it and loved spending time with their grandchildren, but it was difficult for me when I was on call to say to my daughters every night while I was putting them to bed, "If Mommy's not here in the morning, it means that Mommy had to go to work."

It was great when I did have a schedule because I only worked ten days a month, and during those months I was pretty much in complete control of when and how much I worked. If something came up, I could find someone else to take one of my trips; if we needed a little extra money, I could just add a trip. Basically it was a job where you made as much or as little money as you wanted. More important to me was the flexibility it gave that a normal nine-to-five job wouldn't have. When the girls were little, I often gave away flights so I could spend more time with them, and later when they went away to college I added more flights since I didn't have to be home for them anymore.

Of course, the flexibility part of the job only applied to when you had a schedule for that month. When you were on reserve, you had virtually no control of when you flew. One minute you could be sitting at home eating breakfast with your family, and the next you could be on a plane that was taking you to the other side of the world. That's why one of the happiest days of your flight attendant career is when you finally have enough seniority to no longer have to do any reserve at all. For me that took eleven years, and when that day finally came, it felt like I couldn't have asked for anything more.

5.

Passengers

Despite all the horror stories we flight attendants tell about passengers from hell, the overwhelming majority of them are nice, well-behaved people who do not cause any problems whatsoever. As for the few who do become disgruntled, most of the time it is because they have experienced a delay somewhere along the line that will cause them to be late in arriving at their final destination. If the airline was at fault for the delay, disgruntled passengers will sometimes take out their frustration on flight attendants, who, while not being responsible for the delay, represent the face of the company that has caused their inconvenience.

When a passenger does start giving you grief, it is best to first remind yourself that they are not upset because of something you did and apologize to them on behalf of the airline. Sometimes this is enough, but other times you have to give them a little extra attention by asking every so often if they are comfortable or if they need anything and basically try to live up to corporate slogans such as *American Airlines, Doing What We Do Best* SM and *Something Special In The Air*®. If that doesn't work, the best course of action is to just leave them alone as long as they're not disturbing the other passengers or crew members.

Regardless of their level of dissatisfaction, you always have to be very careful about what you say to a disgruntled passenger because you don't know who this person is or how far they are willing to go to prove their point. At 35,000 feet, we don't have the ability to kick someone off the plane. We have to do our best to keep this person in line for the remainder of the flight. If we are unable to do so and the passenger's behavior threatens the safety of the aircraft, the captain then has the option of diverting the flight to the nearest airport, where a team of law enforcement officials will be awaiting our arrival.

Over time, flight attendants develop a sixth sense that becomes so keen that we can tell the moment someone steps on board our plane whether or not they are going to be a difficult passenger. It has nothing to do with race, gender, nationality, height, weight, or any other distinguishing characteristic that can be used to profile someone; it is simply the initial eye contact they make with you when they step on board and how they say hello, if they say anything at all. Still, unless they are combative or visibly inebriated, there is really nothing you can do about passengers you sense are going to be a problem until they do start acting up. If someone starts causing trouble after takeoff, you're stuck having to deal with that person until you're back on the ground. It doesn't matter how long you have been flying, this can be a trying experience.

Usually it is only individuals who give you a difficult time during a flight, but there was one particular route when I first started flying international that was notorious for having entire planes full of rowdy passengers. I worked the last leg of a round trip that originated at JFK and stopped in Aruba and Curacao before returning to JFK. To this day I don't know why it was, but whenever the passengers boarded in Curacao, they brought with them this highly infectious element of rowdiness that was extremely difficult to keep in check once it got started. This was a route that most flight attendants working international knew to stay away from. When you first start flying, you don't have enough seniority to pick and choose all the trips you want to work. Somehow I managed to avoid this particular route for nearly six months before I finally got stuck with it a few days before Christmas.

The passengers who boarded in Curacao were mostly locals, and on this particular flight they were especially festive because they were excited about flying to New York to spend the holidays with their relatives. The crew was a little tired at this point since this was our third flight of the day and we had been dreading this leg of the trip, especially since our supply of soda had run low during the flight to Aruba and we were informed that we would not be able to pick up any more down the line. This wasn't much of a problem between Aruba and Curacao since that was only a forty minute flight, but for the Curacao to JFK leg, we knew it might be. We decided that we would just pour a cup of soda for the passengers rather than giving them the whole can like we normally did. We also had over a hundred special meals ordered which were a bit more appetizing than the regular ones. We had not received a list of the passengers who had ordered them from the ground agents, which was the normal procedure. Without this list, it was impossible to decipher who should receive the special meals. We decided to hand them out first knowing that the passengers would catch on and just say that they had ordered one. We knew that if we asked the passengers who had ordered one, things would quickly get out of hand.

Having only been flying for about year now and still adjusting to the more culturally diverse international flights, I was still a bit green and not really ready to handle a crowd like this, especially on a 747 with close to 400 people on board. I had been assigned to work the first two sections of coach with the purser, and after takeoff he and I were out with the beverage cart when the very first passenger we were about to serve said to me, "I want a Coke, and I want the whole can, so don't tell me I can't have the whole can!"

I was a bit intimidated by this man and I didn't know how to respond to him, I repeated his request to the purser, who had been asking another passenger what they would like to drink.

"I told you, he can't have a whole can," he said to me while pouring the soda from a can that was already open. He handed the cup to the man, who glared at both of us so angrily that I had to look away. The purser paid no attention and pulled the cart away, and fortunately the man said nothing more.

Since departure, the noise level in the cabin had been increasing steadily in conjunction with the amount of alcohol being consumed by the passengers, many of whom brought their own supply. When we brought out the meal carts, everybody suddenly realized how hungry they were and we weren't able to serve them quickly enough. On the bigger planes at the time, we used three carts for the meal service: one for the trays, one for the hot entrées, and one for the beverages. I was working the cart with the entrées, and it didn't take long for the passengers to figure out our ploy regarding the special meals. As soon as we ran out, they started standing in their seats and demanding more special meals. Their voices were competing with each other and mine while I tried to explain that there were none left. I looked around for my crewmembers to give me a little help, but they were nowhere in sight. The noise level continued to escalate to the point where I couldn't even hear myself speak. I thought I was going to start crying, but something else was building inside of me that boiled over when one woman stood up and said with a booming voice, "Could you hurry it up? My people are starving!"

"That's it!" I yelled and slammed my entrée tongs down on the cart, which made a loud clanging noise that startled a few people sitting near me and brought a hush to the cabin. "Lady, if you think you can do this any faster than I can, then by all means, do it!"

On that note, I stormed out of the aisle into the service center and started crying. The purser took one look at the tears rolling down my face and without saying anything, pushed the button for the elevator that led to the lower galley.

"Go downstairs," he said when the doors slid open. "Don't ask any questions, just go downstairs."

I stepped into the elevator and hit the button. The purser disappeared as the doors slid shut and the elevator descended. It was nice and quiet in the elevator until the doors slid open again and the rest of the crew appeared in front of me talking and laughing.

"We were wondering when you were going to show up down here!" one of the other flight attendants said. "We were just talking about how surprised we were that you were still up there!"

They were also talking about how this was one of the worse crowds they had ever seen and how they didn't want to go back up there, which made me feel better knowing that even experienced crews felt the same way I did. After we were through venting, I was able to muster up enough courage to go back up and face what by now might be an angry mob.

When I got back to my cart, I just stood there with arms folded and waited for the passengers to quiet down.

"Now, I'm going to try this again," I said loudly and clearly to the section that had not yet been served, holding my tongs up in the air to show them that I meant business. "But this is the last time. I just want to make it clear that we do not have any special meals left, and if I hear one more complaint out of any of you, then I'm done and the rest of you won't get a meal at all!"

A calm fell over the cabin. When I started serving the meals again, everyone was suddenly very nice and respectful and they quietly thanked me without protest when I handed them their trays. I was truly amazed at how well-behaved they were being after how unruly they had been only moments earlier. It took me a few minutes to believe that I had actually done this. It felt as if I had attained the highest level of flight attendant consciousness and had been empowered with a bold new sense of confidence that would enable me to maintain control of a flight even under the most difficult of circumstances. I also knew that from this moment on, I would no longer be *the new girl*. I could now stand beside any other flight attendant without being intimidated by their experience.

After we finished the last beverage service, a few of us were hanging out in the service center talking about how glad we were that this flight was almost over when a woman came in and introduced herself to the purser. She explained that she was a supervisor from LaGuardia who was doing what is called a "ghost ride" or a "check ride," which is when the airline sends a supervisor to pose as a passenger to make sure that the crew is doing their job properly. They are usually sent from another base so that the crew won't recognize them. Since we were based out of JFK, none of us knew her. My heart started racing when I realized that she may have witnessed my little outburst, but I was ready to defend my actions if necessary. I had fulfilled my ultimate responsibility as a flight attendant by maintaining control of the cabin I had been assigned to despite the difficult situation that the passengers had created.

"We've heard about these flights at LaGuardia," she said, "but never in my wildest dreams did I imagine they were this bad. I just wanted to let you know that you are all getting a wonderful report, and, as far as I'm concerned, my ghost ride is officially over. So, I would like a Bloody Mary, please, because I really need one after this flight!"

On May 25, 1979, American Airlines flight 191, a DC-10 carrying 258 passengers and 13 crew members, was in its takeoff roll at O'Hare International Airport in Chicago when the number one engine separated from the aircraft. The plane managed to get 400 feet off the ground before plummeting into a mobile home park, killing everyone on board and two people on the ground. It was a horrific crash that received extensive media attention and raised serious concerns about the safety of air travel, and it gave me a new awareness as to the dangers of my profession, especially since I often flew in DC-10s.

Tragedies such as this tend to serve as a reminder of the things that are truly important while exposing the relative insignificance of everyday concerns that so often dominate our lives. Afterwards, I couldn't stop thinking about all those people who stepped on board that plane without having the slightest idea that they were about to die, and about how their loved ones must have felt when they heard the news. I also couldn't help thinking that it easily could have been me. I may have even flown on that very plane, or, if it hadn't crashed on that particular day, could have been assigned to it at some point in the future with that engine still at risk of falling off.

It was also around this time that I found out I was pregnant with Kirsten, which further changed my outlook on my profession and my life. When I realized that it was no longer just me going up in the air, I started to question whether or not I should keep flying. This decision weighed on my mind every time I went to work, and now that I clearly recognized what was important, I started becoming less tolerant of pettiness.

A few months after the crash, I was working the number one position on a flight to Aruba when one of the other flight attendants approached me about a young lady who was giving her a difficult time.

"Jean, I can't deal with her anymore," she said. "She's impossible! Would you go to talk to her?"

"What seems to be the problem?"

Apparently this attractive young lady, who appeared to be in her early twenties, had been told by the agent who booked the flight that there would be cottage cheese served with her special meal. She had ordered a vegetarian meal, and since it was a breakfast flight, we served her cereal and toast. What the agent neglected to tell her was that the food cycle changed every month. While there may have been cottage cheese on the menu when the flight was booked, there wasn't during the month that the flight actually took place.

After being handed her meal, the young lady started complaining about the lack of cottage cheese on her tray. The flight attendant repeatedly explained that we simply did not have any cottage cheese on the plane and that she was sorry about being told by the agent that there would be, but this young lady was relentless. Finally the flight attendant became so frustrated that she came to me. With my own passengers to take care of and more important matters on my mind, I wasn't too thrilled about the prospect of explaining that the crew working this flight had not been trained to make cottage cheese materialize out of thin air.

Despite what I had already been told about this young lady, I went back there with my friendly flight attendant smile and asked her what the problem was.

"The problem is," she said, her hand extended to show me her meal, "the lack of cottage cheese on my tray."

"I'm afraid we don't have any cottage cheese anywhere on this plane," I politely explained.

"When I booked this flight, I was guaranteed that cottage cheese would be served with my meal. Now I would like to know where it is. I don't happen to see it on my tray. Do you see any cottage cheese on my tray?"

I was somewhat taken aback by her obstinacy, so I just stared at her for a moment to see if she was playing some sort of game with me, but her expression seemed to indicate that she would settle for no less than having me magically produce the cottage cheese she so desperately craved.

"Listen," I said, "I am only going to explain this once. At 35,000 feet, I cannot produce something that is not on the aircraft. If I had it, believe me, I would give it to you, but right now I can't just step out to 7-Eleven and pick some up. So, what else can I do to make you happy?"

"I want restitution," she said.

"Restitution?" I said incredulously. "You want restitution? Alright. I believe that can be arranged."

I turned to the passengers sitting in the section and asked for their attention, but just about everyone within earshot was already listening anyway.

"I've shopped for cottage cheese in the supermarket," I said, "but I don't always pay close attention to prices, so I was wondering if any of you can help me out. Can somebody tell me what a quart of cottage cheese goes for these days?"

People started calling out prices much like the audience does during the showcase showdown on *The Price is Right*, and eventually it was decided that $1.50 was a fair price.

"So," I said, turning back to the young lady, "if I gave you $1.50 out of my own wallet, would that make you happy?"

By now she was staring out the window and refused to look up at me.

"Alright then," I said after it became clear that I was not going to get a response. "But I have to tell you, miss, that if the only thing in your life you have to worry about is the lack of cottage cheese on your breakfast tray, you are one very lucky lady!"

My two cents must have been enough because she did not accept the $1.50. The other passengers cheered and applauded, and I responded with a shrug and said, "I tried!" I really didn't enjoy embarrassing her like that, but she had it coming. And maybe it taught her to treat people with a little more respect, or at the very least to bring her own cottage cheese the next time she flew somewhere!

Flying can be very stressful when things don't go right, but most people understand that things such as delays are common in the industry and just accept it as part of the experience, even if the airline does happen to be at fault. Still, some people just can't resist the urge to voice their displeasure at airline personnel when they encounter a delay, while others silently decide to choose another carrier the next time they fly. Every once in a while, however, someone comes along whose frustration is so extreme that they wind up endangering the lives of innocent people while exacting their revenge on the cause of their inconvenience.

During the summer of 1986, I worked an afternoon flight to San Juan and was scheduled to work the flight back to New York that night. It was one of those times of year when airlines oversell their flights by a certain percentage based on the average number of ticketed passengers who hadn't been showing up for that same flight in previous weeks. Unfortunately, that flight back to New York was one of few where everybody who bought tickets did show up. This meant that some of them were going to be left behind.

I was working the number two position on this flight and was sitting in the galley jump seat at the back of the plane. After pushing back from the gate, we stopped and just sat there. This was a little unusual, but didn't seem like anything to be alarmed about. After sitting there for ten minutes, however, I called the number one up front and asked him what was going on.

"There's been a bomb threat to the aircraft," he said.

"What?" I said. "When were you going to let me know?"

"I was waiting to hear back from the captain. When I did, then I was going to inform the crew."

Air traffic control had radioed the captain and said there had been a direct bomb threat to our aircraft and asked him if he wanted to either proceed as normal or evacuate the aircraft. The captain responded by saying, "Okay, I'll proceed as normal if you want to come down here and join me!"

For an aircraft evacuation at an airport, the plane has to be moved as far away from the terminal and the other planes as possible. The captain steered the aircraft to the edge of the tarmac next to the area just beyond Luis Muñoz Marín International Airport known as "Sewer Lake," and the ground crew followed with a ramp stand that the passengers would use to deplane.

We announced to the passengers that there was a problem with the plane and that we were going to evacuate, but we did not specifically mention the bomb threat because we didn't want to cause a panic. That might have helped in the end because this crowd was a bit too calm, which made it more difficult for us. Our job during an evacuation is to get the passengers off the aircraft as quickly as possible. Because they weren't aware of the urgency of the situation, however, they got up and started gathering their things as if we had just arrived at our destination. We had to let them know that it was imperative that they exit the plane as quickly as possible.

"Move it! Move it! Shut that bin! Just leave your belongings and get off the plane! Move it!"

When they finally got the message, they couldn't move anyway because there was only one set of stairs, which caused the evacuation to take far longer than it should have. If this had been training, the instructors probably would have made us do it over again. We did eventually get everyone off the plane, and, after checking to make sure that no one was left, the crew deplaned as well.

Two buses eventually arrived to start bringing the passengers back to the terminal. This also took a while because there were only so many passengers that could fit on each bus. The tarmac was pitch black except for the lights of the aircraft, and at one point I turned around and looked up at this enormous plane hovering over us, which is when it finally hit me that this thing could explode at any second. Suddenly I became terribly frightened. I realized that I didn't have my purse with me. Somehow this left me feeling very vulnerable.

My friend Peter from training was also working this flight, so I said to him, "I'm going back on board—I forgot my purse!"

"What are you, nuts?" he said.

"I need my stuff! I don't have any of my belongings with me! I can't even buy a soda if I wanted to!"

"Keiser, I'll buy you a soda if you really want one, so don't worry about it. Are you really that crazy to risk your life just for your purse?"

I knew he was right, but I also knew he didn't fully comprehend I needed to have my stuff with me at all times because without it, I felt totally unprepared for anything else that might occur.

Meanwhile, there was a lot of confusion with the buses, and the fact that many of the passengers only spoke Spanish didn't make the situation any easier. There was also an unaccompanied child on the flight who we had lost track of. That was a harrowing moment. One thing you do not want to do is lose an unaccompanied child! Fortunately, one of the other flight attendants found her in the crowd, and we kept her within arms reach throughout the rest of the ordeal.

Finally, after all the passengers were bused back to the terminal, we were taken to an employee area and were informed that they were going to bring out the bomb-sniffing dogs. This process took several hours.

They had to take all the luggage off the plane for the dogs to sniff and then they had to sniff the entire plane. Eventually, we got word that all was clear and the plane was declared safe for travel.

Despite the reassurances of the security officials, the dogs, and the captain, I was worried that they might have missed something and hesitated before deciding to get back on that plane. In the end I figured that I had to get home somehow, and this was the quickest way. Times were different back then too—this was a couple of years before terrorists had blown up Pan Am flight 103 over Lockerbie, Scotland and long before September 11. Something like this was more likely to be considered a hoax, whereas today it would not.

We later found out that the threat was made from a pay phone in the lounge area of the terminal, which all but confirmed our suspicion that the guilty party was a disgruntled passenger who had gotten bumped from the flight. I understand that people get frustrated, and hey, it's frustrating for us too, but I don't understand how someone can go as far as endangering the lives of not only everybody on the plane, but also the ground rescue personnel who had to rush out there, all because of a simple inconvenience. This is precisely why in the new age of terrorism; your guard is on alert concerning all passengers who board your plane. You hope and pray that each and every flight does not have any passengers with ill intent.

On occasion, there is the unusual experience of recognizing a passenger you've never actually met. A commercial airliner is one of the few places in society where everyday people get to share the same space with the rich and famous. When celebrities do step on board your plane, it is somewhat deceiving. Having seen and read about famous celebrities, you form an opinion about them before ever meeting them. More often than not, they turn out to be completely different than those opinions that you formed. In a way, you have to be even more careful and not let your preconceived notions of them interfere with your professional judgment.

In the early '80s, I was assigned to work the first class section on a flight to St. Maarten, and while the flight was boarding, I was informed by the agent at the gate that Howard Stern and his now ex-wife Alison were about to board the plane. This was when he first went on the air in New York and he wasn't as famous as he is today. I had heard his show a few times driving home from work in the afternoon and thought that if in person he was anything like he was on the radio, I was in for a long flight. As it turned out, they were two of the nicest, loveliest people, and Howard was very funny, but in a much tamer way than he was on his show. At the time, I hadn't met any real celebrities and was under the impression that they were all pushy, demanding people, but the Sterns weren't like that in the least. In fact, they didn't ask for a single thing during the entire flight, and they even brought their own food! If all passengers were like them, my job would be a piece of cake.

And then there was a famous rock star of the '60's. He boarded a flight I was working from Barbados to New York, and he was traveling by himself except for a kitten he had found on the street somewhere in Barbados that he was taking back to the States. At first, he seemed like a nice, down-to-earth guy, and when he was boarding he was laughing and joking with the crewmembers. Before takeoff, several of us gathered around and commented how cute the kitten was, and he seemed happy to show it to us and was very genial. But, as soon as we were up in the air and he took his first sip of ginger ale and Jack Daniels, he instantly transformed into this nasty, vile man. He was finishing his drinks so quickly that I couldn't keep up with him, and each time he drained his glass he would demand another. He became so drunk that I couldn't understand half of what he said (which probably wasn't such a bad thing), and if he were any other passenger I would have cut him off a lot sooner. He was very intimidating and at one point I went up to the flight deck to talk to the captain about him. As I started to enter the cockpit, he started yelling at me to serve him another drink. Clearly he had had too much already!

"Excuse me," I said to him, on the verge of losing my cool. "*I'm* the one in charge here! You don't tell me what I can and can't do!"

Finally, just to shut him up, I started serving him cups of ginger ale with just a drop of Jack Daniels on top so that he would taste the liquor without becoming more inebriated. This kept him quiet until we finally landed. He was one of the worst passengers I ever had to deal with, so bad that after we landed in New York I seriously considered having him arrested. I even followed him off the plane and onto the jet bridge, but at the last minute I changed my mind because I was thinking, *Can you really call the police on a rock star?* So I just let it go, which was probably for the best because he wasn't worth all the procedures I would have had to go through for taking such an extreme measure, and it was probably punishment enough that he had to live with himself, although I felt sorry for that little kitten.

Another time, I was assigned to work first class on a flight to Zurich when I found out that Ivana Trump was going to be on board.

The agent told me that she would be boarding ahead of all the other passengers, which made me think that I was going to be given a laundry list of special instructions about how to treat her. Honestly, I had no idea what she was going to be like. This wasn't long after she and Donald had divorced, but I hadn't followed the story very closely and didn't think she was anything special whenever I saw her on TV or in the newspapers, so I decided to pretend that she was just another passenger.

In person, however, she was stunningly beautiful and had a presence about her that was difficult to ignore. Still, I thought someone of her social standing would be difficult to deal with, but she actually turned out to be a true "lady" and we chit-chatted throughout the flight. She told me that she was on her way to St. Moritz for a ski holiday with her children and that they were already there waiting for her. The entire time that I spent with her I kept thinking, *what was a classy lady like you doing with "The Donald" in the first place?* At the time I wasn't a big fan of Donald Trump and thought he was just some ruthless, powerful businessman who got whatever he wanted, but since then I have become a fan of *The Apprentice* and think he's actually a pretty cool guy.

Another truly classy lady was Princess Margaret of Great Britain. I was an extra for that flight from Barbados to London so I was just kind of along for the ride, but it was exciting to find out that we were going to have an actual princess on board. Of course, I wasn't familiar with Princess Margaret or the royal family and had this idea that princesses were all young and beautiful and had to be rescued from castle towers by knights in shining armor, so I was a little let down when she turned out to be a little older and a little heavier than I thought she would be. She wasn't really *old*, but she seemed so to me because I was in my early twenties and she was in her fifties. Still, she was very lovely, and regal-she just wasn't what I imagined a real princess would look like.

Normally Princess Margaret wouldn't be flying on a commercial jetliner, but she had apparently been on vacation in Barbados with a gentleman friend with whom she had had a tiff and was not willing to wait for the royal jet to come pick her up. Before the flight, ground personnel gave us a crash course on royal etiquette, the instructions were not to speak directly to the princess but instead address her personal assistant. They also informed us that her bodyguards and assistants were to occupy the entire first class cabin with her and that under no circumstances outside of an emergency were any of the other passengers permitted to step foot in first class.

The airport in Barbados did not have jet bridges at the time, so ramp stairs were used for boarding instead. When it was time for the princess to board, her staff rolled out a red carpet on the tarmac and gave her an honor guard salute which made me wonder if she actually enjoyed all this ceremony every time she did something simple like board an airplane or if she secretly longed to live a normal life and be treated like a regular person. It was an impressive sight nonetheless. The rest of the flight was uneventful and we really didn't do anything out of the ordinary. The first class cabin was especially quiet.

Several weeks later, a letter handwritten by Princess Margaret on Buckingham Palace stationery arrived at American Airlines headquarters thanking the crew for their exemplary service. It didn't seem like we did anything special. In fact, we had pretty much just left her alone during the whole flight. Still, it seemed like an exceptionally considerate thing to do. There are so many occasions when you go out of your way for passengers who don't give you as much as a thank you as they're leaving the plane and here was this real-life princess who took the time to write a letter of thanks for simply doing our jobs. That really impressed me. Rare gestures such as this serve as a reminder that for every drunk rock star in the world, there is someone like Princess Margaret to make up for it.

6.

Both Feet on the Ground

After nearly a decade of flying all over the world to places that most people only dream about, my career started to become a blur of airport terminals and hotel lobbies. Sometimes I would wake up in a dark hotel room and have to think about what country I was in and after I had that straightened out, I would then have to figure out where in the world I would be spending the next night. I often didn't know if I was coming or going. It was beginning to wear on me. I needed some stability in my life. I needed something that resembled a routine.

Every year when I went back to the flight academy in Dallas for our annual F.A.A.-mandated "Emergency Procedural Training" ("E.P.T.") and "Recurrent Ditching Training" ("R.D.T.") review courses, I thought about how much I enjoyed my initial flight attendant training and how someday I would like to be a new-hire instructor. One night I mentioned this in passing to Doug and while I wasn't seriously considering it at the time, he knew that I was burnt out from flying and asked me if I really wanted to do it.

"The position is in Dallas," I reminded him.

"I know," he said. "But if this is something you really want to do, then I'm willing to move to Dallas."

"What about your job?"

"My company has offices in Dallas-I can transfer."

That conversation was all it took to get the ball rolling. It got to the point where we actually put our house up for sale. As soon as I saw that real estate sign planted on the front lawn, however, I didn't feel right about it. At the time we had just had Kirsten. My father, whom I was very close to, was not in good health, and I didn't want to move his only grandchild fifteen-hundred miles away. Then I became pregnant with Kelly, which is when I realized that it just wasn't meant to be.

So I kept on flying. The thrill of being in places such as Rome or Brussels or Punta Cana was replaced by a desire to be closer to home. I started thinking about how nice it would be to have a job in New York where, even if I was at work, I would at least only be an hour drive away rather than stuck in a hotel room on the other side of the world. I still loved to fly and I didn't want to give it up for good, but I needed a break from it.

That break didn't come for another ten years. In the spring of 1992, I heard about an opening with the airline for an instructor position in New York. While many of the drills for the E.P.T. and R.D.T. courses required use of the flight simulators down at the academy in Dallas, some sections of the program could be taught in a classroom. These classes were held at local bases. In New York, they were held at JFK. I went ahead and applied for the position and a couple of months later, I was accepted.

After eighteen years of flying, I was very excited about the opportunity of doing something different. I was also very nervous because my students weren't going to be new hires who didn't yet know anything about the job. They would be my peers. It was important to me that I earn their respect as an instructor. Though it would be a challenge to teach people things they should already know, I had accumulated a lot of knowledge over my career that I wanted to share with my colleagues. Knowledge that might prove useful to even the most experienced flight attendants. If nothing else, my ultimate goal as an instructor was for my students to walk out of that classroom having learned something.

There were four instructors for each class who took turns teaching the different sections. When you weren't teaching, you were either doing paperwork or waiting your turn to go up in front of the class. I was very nervous on my first day. About five minutes before I was supposed to be at the podium, I decided that I had better go to the bathroom so I wouldn't have to during my lecture.

That day, I was wearing a one piece outfit that was like a jumpsuit, which meant that I had to practically get undressed in order to use the facilities. After I went, I was putting the outfit back on when one of the sleeves fell into the bowl and got soaked with toilet water. For a moment I thought I was going to scream. Instead I hurried over to the sink; half-undressed and frantically tried to wash out the smell with hot water and soap from the dispenser. Afterwards, I held it under the hand dryer, but the blast of hot air only seemed to intensify the odor. I finished getting dressed and stared at myself in the mirror wondering how in my present condition was I going to be able to stand in front of a room full of people and teach. For the past several days, all I had been thinking about was how cool, calm, and collected I needed to be when I walked into that classroom, and here I was with less than a minute to go a total mess and reeking of urine!

I knew as I walked into the classroom that I looked like a nervous wreck, not to mention being partially soaked. I figured that the best course of action was humor. I introduce myself and simply told the class what happened. A lot of times I find laughter to be the perfect tie-breaker.

"For those of you who don't know me," I said, "my name is Jean Keiser. I'm going to be totally honest with you. Today is my first day of teaching, and a few minutes ago I went to use the ladies room and my sleeve fell into the toilet bowl. Now, in addition to being a nervous wreck, I smell of urine. So, if you think you smell anything, it's not the person sitting next to you, it's me."

The class laughed, which calmed my nerves just enough so that I was able to get through that first section without further incident. In fact, dropping my sleeve in the toilet may have been a good thing in a way because from then on I went to work knowing that there weren't many more embarrassing things that could happen. Still, I had my moments, especially at the beginning when I was trying so hard to be the perfect instructor that I sometimes lost focus.

Early on in my teaching, there was one particular group of students that made me a little more nervous than usual, and that was because my friend George was in that class. While I like George, he does take the job very seriously and he knows *everything. This makes him a good flight attendant to work with.* When you have to stand up in front of a classroom and try to teach something to someone who probably knows more about what you are trying to teach than you do, the task can seem rather daunting. To make matters worse, a few of George's friends signed up to take the class that same day. There was a whole group of them looking up at me in their seats eagerly waiting for me to pass along my flight attendant wisdom.

That day, I was teaching the section that covered the proper way to recruit and brief passengers as assistants for a planned evacuation. After the assistants have been recruited, the flight attendant has to read them instructions from a briefing card, show them the diagrams on the card, and then ask them a couple of questions to make sure that they understand what they are supposed to do. It is a rather straightforward procedure and before class, I was relieved that this was one of the demonstrations I would be doing because all I really had to do was read from a card.

My lecture seemed to start out okay and while I was speaking, I kept reminding myself to stay focused. I became so focused on staying focused, however, that I lost focus of what I was actually saying and after several minutes, I noticed that everyone in the room was looking at me with puzzled expressions. At first I thought that maybe I was talking too fast, so I slowed down and tried speaking more clearly. In doing so, I realized that what I was saying wasn't making any sense. Finally George stopped me, got out of his seat and joined me in front of the class.

"You know what, Jean?" he said, taking the briefing card from my hand and flipping it over. "Why don't we try starting on page one."

Everyone laughed, and I was so embarrassed that I wanted to run out of the room and drive straight home. But the tension I had been feeling since stepping into the classroom that morning had been broken and afterwards everyone in the room seemed more relaxed, especially me.

"You know what, guys?" I said, holding up the card. "You've all done this demonstration plenty of times much better than I just did, so we can consider this part of the class done. Or does anyone want me to go over it again?"

Fortunately they had mercy on me and didn't make me attempt it again.

"Alright then," I said. "But if any one of your critique sheets says that I didn't do this demonstration correctly, just keep in mind that we have your addresses on file, I can easily find out where you live!"

After I got the hang of teaching, I absolutely loved it. I had a lot of fun doing it and I got to see just about everyone I had worked with. All the JFK based flight attendants had to pass through the class sooner or later. In addition the woman who was my supervisor was wonderful. Only a couple of weeks after I started, my mother called and said that my father had been taken to the hospital and was in intensive care. Even though I had just started the job, my supervisor told me to get out of there and go see my father. They would cover for me until I was ready to come back.

Later that summer, my father passed away. I shuffled my scheduled teaching days around so that I had a stretch of six consecutive days off. By then he was at home since there was no point in him being at the hospital. After the phone call from my mother telling me the news about my father passing, I drove to their house. While I was driving, I started thinking about how he had instilled his strong German work ethic upon us when we were growing up. I heard myself say out loud in the car, "It figures that you would die on my first day off, God forbid that I should have to miss a day of work for your funeral!"

When I got back to work the following Monday, my supervisor asked me if I needed any more time off, but I told her I was fine. I knew my father wouldn't have wanted me to miss a day of work on his account.

Although I didn't really miss flying at first, I did have to adjust to working a regular work week. This was very different from my usual flight schedules. The hours were scheduled to be from seven in the morning to three in the afternoon, four days a week. You were scheduled to work either Monday through Thursday or Tuesday through Friday and you were required to arrive before the class started so you could pull up the class roster for that day. In the afternoon when the class was over you had to re-administer the tests for the people who didn't pass with 90% or higher. Once the tests were completed, the F.A.A. qualifications had to be updated in the computer for the flight attendants and then the classroom had to be set up for the next day. It was usually well after four o'clock by the time I was finished. This put my drive home during rush hour. A normal 25 minute ride could take well over an hour. When I got home I had to accomplish all the requirements of a working mom. I had to drive the girls to their dance lessons; or any other activity they were scheduled for that day, prepare dinner and lunches and get their clothes ready for the next day as well as my own. It was exhausting! As a flight attendant, I usually selected afternoon and night trips and only worked about ten or twelve days a month, many of those days being on weekends. This gave me the opportunity to do all my errands and shopping during the week when the stores weren't so crowded, and with Doug and my parents helping out when I had to work, it wasn't so bad. After experiencing this more traditional schedule, however, I had newfound respect for working mothers, especially single working mothers who didn't have nearly as much help as I did.

After instructing for three years, I decided that it would be best for my family and myself if I started flying again. As it turned out, flying all over the world actually allowed me to spend more time at home, and the schedule was much more flexible. I could easily trade my trips around if I needed some time off, which was not a possibility as an instructor.

Besides, that nine-to-five routine is difficult. Doug had teased me during my teaching that I was finally finding out what it was like to have a real job. I used to respond by telling him that it wasn't as easy as he thought working irregular schedules and flying all over the world, dealing with jetlag and sleeping in hotels. I knew very well how lucky I was!

Since then, all the training classes have been moved back to Dallas, which is disappointing because I would love to teach again now that the girls are all grown up and I am nearing retirement. When I went back to flying in 1995, though, with the girls growing up so fast, I wanted to be at home as much as possible. I didn't want to miss a thing, and the flexibility of the flight attendant schedule would allow me to be there whenever something came up.

At that time, I was also beginning to miss flying. That had been my calling all along, and there was only so long I could stay in one place with both feet on the ground.

7.

Combustible Hotels

Some people think that I am incredibly unlucky because of the things I've been through during my career, the hijacking in particular. Others think that I am actually very lucky to have survived such experiences. Honestly, I don't know if it's good luck or bad luck, bad timing coupled with good fortune, twist of fate, matter of circumstance, or the alignment of the universe. What I do know is that some things in life are beyond explanation, and when you do encounter a situation that defies probability, it is usually best to just accept it as is and move on. If you spend too much time trying to figure it out, you're only going to drive yourself crazy.

For example, what are the odds of experiencing two hotel fires in the same city almost exactly a year apart? Most frequent travelers go their whole lives without their hotel going up in flames, yet in 1996, I experienced the first of two blazes at a hotel where I was staying in Miami.

This first one took place at the Hyatt. My mother happened to be in Florida sharing a condo with my best friend Patty's mother-in-law. Patty is based in Miami and at that time lived in Jupiter, which was eighty five miles north of Miami. Our layover hotel was in Key Biscayne. Patty and her husband, along with the two moms, decided to drive down and have dinner with me. I was only going to be there for one night, so we decided to go down to South Beach for dinner. What we hadn't taken into account was that it was Saturday night, and South Beach was a little too crowded and wild for a nice quiet dinner. We decided to go back to the Hyatt, which had a restaurant known for its five star cuisine.

As we neared the hotel, however, several of the roads were blocked off by police cars and there were fire trucks and ambulances everywhere with their lights flashing. Bobby tried to find a different route to the hotel, but all the roads leading to it had been blocked off. A policeman informed us that there was a fire at the hotel, but he said it wasn't too serious and that they had it under control. I explained that I was staying at the hotel. He said that they would probably be letting people back into their rooms soon and that I could walk back if I wanted to, but they weren't allowing anyone to drive into the area just yet in case any emergency vehicles needed to get through.

At that point, it was getting late and we were already weary of driving around looking for somewhere to eat, so I suggested that we give up on the idea of dinner and that they just head back home. I knew my mother was probably getting tired and Patty's mother-in-law as well. With a two hour drive ahead of them, they should get started back. I had to get up early the next morning anyway, and since the fire at the hotel didn't sound too serious, I could just head over there and wait until it was safe to go back up to my room. The others looked at me like I was crazy to spend the night in a burning hotel, but I wouldn't take no for an answer.

"I'll be fine!" I insisted.

I thought the hotel was only a few blocks away, but it turned out to be a little further than I thought, about half a mile. As I got closer, I started to smell smoke, and when I was making my way up the walk in front of the hotel, several paramedics emerged from the lobby struggling to carry a heavyset woman on a stretcher into a waiting ambulance. They didn't quite make it and dropped her on the sidewalk. I started to get worried that this fire was a little more serious than the policeman had told us, so I headed inside to see if I could find out what was going on.

The lobby was packed with hundreds of people who had been evacuated from their rooms; many of them senior citizens who had just returned from or were about to set sail on one of the cruise ships based nearby. The smell of smoke was much stronger in here, and, not sure of what else to do, I wandered aimlessly through the lobby looking at the myriad of confused faces that didn't seem to notice me floating by. I had been up since four that morning and it was now around ten at night. Suddenly I was hit with a wave of exhaustion so powerful that it felt like I was going to pass out on the spot. Fortunately, I was able to locate a vacant chair nearby, and, despite all the noise and activity around me, I fell asleep immediately. Maybe the fumes had affected me in some way, because I wasn't even concerned that the building was on fire and that falling asleep inside of it probably wasn't a very wise thing to do.

It turned out that the fire started in the kitchen of the restaurant where we had planned on eating, and at around two in the morning an announcement was made that we could go back to our rooms. I was in such a deep sleep that I didn't even hear the announcement, but one of the hotel employees who had seen me conked out on the chair for the past several hours woke me up and told me I could go back up to my room.

When I got back upstairs, there were several messages from Patty. I called her back and jokingly said, "Some friends you are, dropping me off and leaving me at a burning building!" Patty laughed knowing that I was okay now. She said that they had been worried sick since returning home because they hadn't been able to get in touch with me. They were even considering driving back to Miami until I called. She said that they hadn't wanted to leave me there like that in the first place and felt bad about it all the way home, but I had been so insistent that they didn't know what else to do.

After getting off the phone with Patty and finally climbing into bed, I couldn't fall asleep. Despite having been off-duty, I was a little uneasy at my failure to recognize how dangerous the situation had been, which is one of the things I get paid to do up in the air. From that night on, I began taking fire safety very seriously and started memorizing exit locations whenever I checked into a hotel. I didn't think for one minute that doing this would come in handy so soon afterwards!

About a year later, I was back in Miami on another layover and had made plans to have a late lunch/early dinner with Patty since she was scheduled to work a flight to London later that evening. After checking in at the hotel on Collins Avenue, I went up to my room and changed into a bathing suit and shorts. I was planning on sitting by the pool for a little while before Patty picked me up, but first I wanted to work on my bid schedule for the following month. As I was doing so, however, I suddenly felt very tired, much like I had during that night at the Hyatt, so I decided to lay down and take a quick nap.

I'm not sure how long I was asleep, but I woke up some time later and the room was muggy and hot. I was groggy and the room was incredibly quiet, which was strange because I could have sworn I turned on the rather noisy air conditioner as soon as I had gotten there. I got out of bed and tried to turn it back on, but it wasn't working. The lamp wasn't working either, nor was the television, so I called the front desk.

Instead of saying hello, however, the lady who answered the phone frantically asked me what I was still doing in my room.

"Excuse me?" I said.

"The hotel is on fire!"

"What?"

"The hotel is on fire! Everyone has been evacuated!"

"Well, nobody told me!"

"What floor are you on?"

"Nineteen."

"Oh my God! The fire is directly below you! You have to get out immediately!"

Since I had memorized the exits when I checked in, I knew that the closest one was directly to the right of my room. When I opened the door to the stairwell, however, it was pitch black in there and very hot. I got really nervous because I knew the elevators were not an option in a fire and that nineteen floors were probably well beyond the reach of a fire truck ladder or a cherry picker. My only hope was the stairwell at the opposite end of the hallway. I started running towards the illuminated red letters of the "EXIT" sign at the other end trying to figure out what I would do if that exit was blocked too, but I stopped cold when I thought I heard a voice behind me.

"Miss?" said an elderly woman standing beside an elderly man just outside the open door of her room. "Miss, what is happening here?"

"Wait right there," I said and continued towards the exit to make sure that we could get out that way. When I opened the stairwell door, there was bright sunlight coming through the windows and there wasn't any smoke.

I hurried back to where the elderly woman was waiting, the man having apparently gone back inside the room. I quickly explained that the hotel was on fire and we had to evacuate down the stairs immediately.

"Jack!" she called into the room. "Jack, we have to leave! The hotel is on fire!"

This fire occurred not long after I had seen *Titanic*, which was still in the theaters, so, as we were slowly descending the stairs and she kept saying his name over and over again, I kept thinking of Leonardo DiCaprio and wondered why I couldn't wind up with a Jack like him. This Jack was ninety years old and all crooked!

It took a while, but we eventually made it safely to the huge set of center stairs that led down to the lobby that looked a little bit like the grand staircase on the *Titanic*. There were several fire trucks parked right out front, and, just like the fire last year, there were hundreds of people in the lobby, only here a section of it was roped off and a large group of senior citizens was sitting there playing BINGO! Jack and his wife decided to head over and join them, and I stood at the top of the stairs watching in disbelief as the white-haired players calmly stamped their BINGO cards and anxiously awaited the next number to be called, seeming not to mind that the building was burning above us!

Meanwhile, my fellow crew members were nowhere in sight. I thought I knew exactly where to find them, though. I went out back to the pool, which had been roped off because of the fire. Sure enough, there they were sitting on the deck drinking beers. They were a junior crew in their twenties and they didn't seem too concerned that the hotel was on fire or about anything else for that matter. I said, "Guys, we can't stay here! We have to go to another hotel!"

"Okay, Jean," one of them said. "We'll let you take care of it."

I gave them a reproachful look before going back around front, where another crew from American had just been dropped off. They were being told by the hotel manager that they couldn't stay there. I went up to the manager and told him I was part of another crew already staying there, and he said that I would have to call the airline to make arrangements to move to another hotel.

"But we have to go up to our rooms and get our belongings." I said.

"Oh, no no no," he said. "You can't go up there!"

"Excuse me," I said, starting to get little frustrated with the lack of cooperation I had encountered during the last five minutes, "we have to work tomorrow-we can't work a flight in our bathing suits! We have to get up to our rooms and get our stuff!"

Finally, the manager said that he would go talk to the captain of the fire department, who came over a few minutes later and instructed me to gather my crew and that each of us would be escorted up to our rooms by a fireman.

"That'll work just fine," I said, liking the sound of that.

I went back out to the pool and told the crew that we had to go up and get our stuff, but they had gotten a little too comfortable where they were. When they made no move to get up, I said, "We have to do it *now* because we have to go to another hotel!" Once they saw that I meant business, they finally got the message and went back around front with me.

I was assigned this gorgeous fireman who escorted me all the way up the nineteen flights of stairs. Like a true gentleman, he waited out in the hallway while I gathered my stockings, my uniform, and the rest of my belongings that were scattered about the room. Once I had all my belongings, he escorted me back down the stairs, and this time I was the slow one because I was pretty tired by now. I didn't mind because it meant that I got to spend more time with this fireman. When we reached the *Titanic* staircase, I couldn't help but feel a little like Rose when she finally joined Jack at the end of the movie when everyone was standing around applauding. Only here, instead of clapping, they were yelling BINGO!

As we were walking down the stairs, my friend Patty walked into the lobby and stopped short when she saw us.

"Jean!" she said, "what is this? Every time you're in Miami, your hotel goes on fire!"

"I know," I said, "but look-at least this time I got a really cute fireman out of it!"

I love Miami. It's a great city. Because of all the flights to the Caribbean that I have worked in my career, I've probably had more layovers in Miami than anywhere else in the world. I am not superstitious nor do I believe in having bad luck or bad karma. Yet, after what I have been through since then I can't help but wonder if those two fires were not just an unlikely coincidence, but actually a warning of things to come.

8.

José

"What are you eating?" José asked.

"Cereal," I said.

"What kind of cereal?"

"High fiber cereal."

"Why are you eating high fiber cereal?"

"Because I'm on a diet."

"Why are you on a diet?"

"José, if you ask me one more question, you're going to be wearing this high fiber cereal!"

It was a few days before Thanksgiving in 2000, and we were working the first leg of flight 1291 to Port Au Prince, Haiti, with a brief stop in Miami. We had departed from JFK early that morning. Since I am not a morning person, I bid the number two position so I wouldn't have the responsibility of being purser for the month. José wound up in the number one position, which he enjoyed very much because he took great pride in being the flight attendant in charge. So much so, in fact, that he had actually laminated all of his training manuals and brought them with him on every trip.

"Is this what you do with your days off?" I kidded him during a previous trip when I first saw the laminated manuals. "Don't you have better things to do than to sit at home and laminate your training manuals? Don't you have a life?"

José Chiu did actually have a life, a pretty interesting one at that. He loved to travel and loved the outdoors; he was a skier, a mountain-climber, and a kayaker. He had just bought a house that he had completely renovated by himself. He was also engaged and was always proudly showing us pictures of his fiancée, never mind that she was seventeen and still in high school and he was a thirty-four year old flight attendant.

"What is wrong with you?" I would ask every time he showed us new pictures of her. "This girl should be planning her prom, not her wedding!" My youngest daughter was the same age as Jose's girlfriend and I couldn't imagine her getting married to a thirty-four year old man!

Despite his quirks, everybody loved José, and he loved being a flight attendant. He was very well-respected by his colleagues, and he wanted to know everything there was to know about the job. He was the same way with people. He wanted to know everything about the person he was talking to and was always asking questions. He wasn't nosy; he just wanted to make a personal connection with everyone he met.

While his childlike inquisitiveness was one of the most likable aspects of his personality, it sometimes made it difficult to work with him if you were not in the right frame of mind. Instead of taking the hint that you wanted to be left alone, he would only start digging deeper with his endless questions if he knew that he was getting under your skin.

On that particular morning, our flight from New York to Miami was pretty empty, which gave José plenty of time to mingle while I was trying to eat my breakfast. This was my last scheduled trip before Thanksgiving and I had a million things to do that week. The girls were coming home from college and I was planning on giving them a good old-fashioned Thanksgiving dinner with all the fixings since all they had been eating for the past several months was dining hall food and Ramen noodles! On Saturday Doug and I were invited to a wedding that we both were looking forward to. I was a little bit stressed out that morning, and José was doing nothing to help relieve that stress.

"What kind of diet are you on that you have to eat high-fiber cereal?" he asked.

"José, I'm warning you!"

"How does eating high fiber cereal help you lose weight?"

"José!"

The next leg of the trip required us to change planes in Miami to one that was flying in from Orlando. When we got to Miami, however, the aircraft hadn't arrived yet, so I decided to do some Christmas shopping in the terminal while the other crew members got something to eat or took a quick nap in the sleeping lounge. After our plane arrived from Orlando, we found out that it had a mechanical problem and that they would have to retrieve another one from the hangar.

The replacement aircraft was an Airbus A300 that had been in for maintenance, which was nothing unusual because all planes have to be inspected and tweaked after logging a certain number of flight hours. The passengers and crew alike had been growing restless sitting in the terminal for several hours now. Everyone was very relieved to finally be leaving for Port Au Prince after the long delay. With all the safety regulations regarding maintenance checks and inspections and everything else that had to be done before putting an aircraft into service, the thought that this plane might not be airworthy did not cross any of our minds.

After boarding the passengers and taking off, we thought that the worst was finally behind us. A little more than ten minutes into the flight, however, the passenger call bells started ringing and wouldn't stop, even though nobody was pressing them. Then the flight attendant phones started ringing, but nobody was on the other end when we answered. The smoke alarms in the lavatories started going off, but there was no evidence of fire or smoke, although one of the other flight attendants noticed a "mild electrical smell" in one of them. Also, some of the passengers and other crew members were complaining that their ears were beginning to hurt.

Meanwhile up in the cockpit, the captain realized that there was a problem with the automatic pressurization system. He informed the first officer that the plane was depressurizing and instructed him to descend to 10,000 feet from the present altitude of 16,000. He then radioed air traffic control to request permission to return to Miami. Permission was granted, and a few minutes later he announced to the passengers that there was a mechanical problem with the aircraft and that we were returning to Miami. He apologized for the inconvenience and said that the mechanics would attempt to correct the problem as quickly as possible; otherwise, they would bring us a different aircraft.

The passengers were understandably frustrated by yet another delay, especially since nobody knew how long we were going to have to wait in Miami before we got back up in the air. The crew was pretty frustrated too. When the plane touched down, we were all very relieved to be safely back on the ground. We were all aware how serious an in-flight pressurization malfunction can be. With that in mind, it didn't seem all that bad. All we thought that we had to do now was deplane the passengers and then wait in the terminal until the mechanics fixed this plane or brought us another one.

Instead of turning towards the terminal, however, we stopped at the end of the runway and just sat there for what seemed like an eternity. I didn't know what was going on until the captain finally announced over the P.A. system, "Ladies and gentlemen, we will be evacuating this aircraft momentarily. Flight attendants, please stand by for my signal to begin ground emergency evacuation procedures."

There must have been something seriously wrong if we were doing an emergency evacuation, which meant that we were going to have to use the slides. At first I thought this seemed a little extreme since we were already safely on the ground at the airport, but I was unaware that one of the other flight attendants had reported an electrical wire smell in one of the middle lavatories and that up in the cockpit a *cargo compartment loop light* had blinked on indicating that a smoke detector down in one of the cargo holds had detected smoke. The captain radioed the ground controller and said, "We have a fire and we are going to evacuate right here." Prior to landing he had requested fire personnel to check the outside of the plane for any visible evidence for fire, so the fire trucks were already on their way.

When the captain gave the order to evacuate, the adrenaline started surging through my body as I shifted into emergency mode. After making a quick assessment of my surroundings and determining that all was clear, I pulled up on the door handle, but for some reason it wouldn't open. I tried again several more times, but it still wouldn't budge.

"What is wrong with this door?" I said to myself.

I tried disarming the door and then arming it again, but it still wouldn't open. I pulled on the handle several more times until my shoulder started to hurt. Finally I determined that this door was a "blocked exit" and began the "blocked exit procedure," which basically meant that I had to elevate myself on the nearest passenger seat, look for an available exit, and redirect the passengers towards it once I found one. After standing up on the seat, however, I saw the other flight attendants up front directing the passengers towards the back.

"No, don't send them back here!" I called to them. "We don't have any open doors back here either!"

It was a bright, sunny day in Miami. If one of the other doors was open on the plane, I should have been able to see a patch of sunlight coming in, but the entire cabin was dim. When I realized that none of the doors were open, I got off the seat and went back to my door thinking, *I'm going to get this door open if it's the last thing I ever do!* I started pulling up on that door handle as if my life depended on it until finally my arms and shoulders couldn't take it anymore.

Meanwhile, the passengers were all standing in the aisle looking to us for guidance since they had been told to evacuate. I didn't have any answers for them, so I tried not to make eye contact with anyone while I tried to figure out what to do next. In all the training I'd had plus having been an instructor for three years, not once was a "no-exit available" scenario covered. There was no protocol for this situation. Finally, I elevated myself again to see if possibly another door was open when I heard a small explosion towards the front of the aircraft. My ears popped and the cabin became a wind tunnel filled with mist (this is what happens when a plane suddenly depressurizes up in the air).

Since the cabin had apparently been pressurized, I figured that was the reason why the door wouldn't open-there is a safety mechanism that keeps the doors locked when the aircraft is pressurized since sudden depressurization is very dangerous. Now that the cabin was depressurized, however, I thought that if I tried again, it would open and I could start evacuating the passengers. Sure enough, when I pulled up on the handle this time, it opened without difficulty. With the exit now clear, I released the emergency slide and watched it drop out of its compartment and begin to inflate. This process takes less than a minute to complete, but it seemed like an eternity. One gentleman was ready to jump out as soon as I pulled the release.

"Stop!" I said, throwing my arm in front of him like a toll booth gate to prevent him from jumping. I kept my hand there thinking that he would understand that he was not to jump before I gave the sign. The moment I turned my attention to the chaotic scene behind me and started instructing people not to gather their belongings, he stepped around my outstretched arm and jumped anyway. The slide, unfortunately, had not yet fully inflated. While it did help slow his thirty foot descent somewhat, it wasn't enough to keep him from breaking his ankle when he hit the tarmac.

In the meantime, most of the other passengers were still trying to grab their belongings out of the overhead bins, and, similar to the evacuation in San Juan many years earlier, many of them did not speak English. There was so much noise that I figured they probably couldn't hear me anyway, so I used the passenger standing at the front of the line as an example by taking his bag from him and pointing to it while saying, "No bags!" and shaking my head. The slide was inflated by now, so I sent him down. Seeing this passenger disappear out of the plane so suddenly, the other passengers finally started to understand how serious this situation was.

Many people were afraid to jump out of the plane, which was certainly understandable. The slide is at such a steep angle that it doesn't look like it is going to do anything to help break the fall. Even I had forgotten how steep it was. It had been many years since my initial training in Dallas and there you jumped into a padded pit, not a concrete tarmac! I kept yelling "Jump jump jump!" I was hoping that my urgency would help the passengers overcome their fear, which it did for most, but some still balked and needed a little more encouragement. A couple of firemen arrived and started helping out at the bottom. It was important to get the passengers off the bottom of the slide as quickly as possible so that the others coming down wouldn't land on top of each other and start piling up.

One woman stopped at the door with an infant in her arms and was crying, "Baby! Baby!" I told her to wait a moment and called down to the fireman below that this woman was coming down with a baby and to be ready just in case she accidentally let go of it. I was really worried about this because the only help I could offer was to show her how to hold on to the baby as tight as she could. I gave her a little extra time while making sure that they were ready down below, and fortunately she made it down safely. As she was being helped off the slide, she looked up at me gratefully and I realized what a difficult thing that must have been for her to do.

Once we had found a rhythm, we managed to evacuate the remaining passengers rather quickly and then made a sweep of the aircraft to make sure that there were none left on board. After determining that all was clear, Kimberly, the other aft flight attendant, and I went back to our exits. I looked down at the slide and then at all the people scattered about the tarmac looking up at us.

"I guess it's our turn," I said to Kimberly, suddenly realizing that I was probably more nervous than most of the passengers had been. "This is pretty steep." She acknowledged that it was.

Not only was it steep, I was wearing a skirt, so my biggest fear was not so much getting injured from the drop but that my skirt would fly up around my head and show everyone what I was wearing underneath.

"We'd better go now," Kimberly said.

I knew she was right, so I just took a deep breath and held it as if I was jumping into a swimming pool and took the plunge. Following the advice I had given the lady with the baby, I held on to my skirt for dear life and managed to keep my modesty in tact. Kimberly jumped out of her exit and then the captain, who is always the last person to exit the aircraft, appeared at my exit and slid down to complete the evacuation.

Down on the tarmac, I noticed a Haitian woman crying hysterically, so I went over to her to see if there was anything I could do to help. She didn't speak any English and I couldn't figure out what was wrong, but fortunately one of our flight service directors, who is Haitian, came to assist her.

In the meantime, buses started pulling up to bring passengers back to the terminal. One of the flight service directors started giving instructions in Haitian Creole about boarding the buses, which was a big help. Then I spotted the passenger who had jumped out of the plane before the slide had inflated. He was being attended to by a couple of paramedics. I went over to see how he was doing. I told him that he should have waited until I told him to jump which he realized now. I talked to him for a couple of minutes until I heard a commotion over near one of the buses. One of the fireman, apparently aware that the passengers weren't supposed to have taken any of their belongings off the plane, was trying to take a carry-on bag away from an elderly Haitian woman who had managed to sneak it off the aircraft with her. It didn't really matter now because the purpose of leaving the bags on the plane was to make the evacuation go faster. I went over and pulled the fireman aside.

"Look," I said, "if she made it this far with her belongings, let her keep them. Whatever she's got in that bag is pretty important to her, so just let it go and see if there's anyone else who needs help."

He eventually relented, and, after he was gone, the woman thanked me in Creole before proceeding to board the bus. I stood there for a moment and took a deep breath while wondering how much weirder this day was going to get.

While I was looking around to see if anyone else needed any help, I spotted another person on the ground being attended to by some paramedics about fifty feet away. Several of the other flight attendants were over there as well, and it seemed strange. They were so far from everyone else. I started over there to see what was going on, but Marcos, one of the other flight attendants, caught up to me from behind and put his hand on my shoulder, so I stopped.

"Jean," he said. "You don't want to go over there."

"Why not?"

"It's José."

"Well, then he needs our help," I said and proceeded towards him.

After the captain had given the signal to begin the evacuation, José attempted to open the door at the very front of the plane, just as the rest of us had been doing at our assigned doors. At the time none of us were aware that the plane was still pressurized; in fact, not only was it still pressurized, it was over pressurized and the pressure was still rising. The cockpit crew didn't realize this because the cabin altimeter was providing them with misleading information.* The aircraft was like a balloon being filled with too much helium, and, unfortunately for José; his exit is where it popped. The door exploded outward, and he was ejected from the plane onto the tarmac fifty feet away.

He was in bad shape. He had been holding the handle of the door when the explosion occurred, and it was obvious as I approached that he had suffered severe physical trauma. While the paramedics were working on him, an off-duty flight attendant who had been deadheading on the flight was working the *ambu-bag*, a device that covers the victim's mouth and sends oxygen into the lungs.

Martha, another flight attendant, was with him, and she suggested to me that we rub his arms and legs and talk to him so that he knew we were there.

"But Martha," I said. "He's dead."

"Jean, don't say that!"

We got down on our knees and started rubbing him and saying things like, "Hang in there, José," and, "You're not alone," but I was skeptical as to whether it was doing any good. Martha, however, seemed convinced that it was, and after a while I began to think, *what did I know? Maybe he can hear us. Maybe this is making him feel better, and maybe in this age of modern medicine they will be able to save him...*

A short time later another team of medical personnel arrived and thanked us for helping, but asked us to get out of the way. By then, the last of the passengers were boarding the bus, leaving only the flight attendants and emergency personnel out on the tarmac.

Not knowing what else to do but not wanting to leave José, we stood by one of the fire trucks until a medic helicopter arrived and took him away. It was a horrible sight, but then one of the firemen came over to let us know that the medics had managed to get José breathing again. Despite what our eyes had seen, we seized that ray of hope and were determined to cling to it believing that José was going to be okay until somebody told us otherwise.

A short time later, the base manager for American arrived and apologized for taking so long to get out there, explaining that she had to wait to get clearance from the N.T.S.B. before she was allowed out on the tarmac. We were then taken by shuttle van to a conference room in the terminal, where the press had already found out about the accident and were taking pictures and asking for comments. Inside the conference room we were administered drug tests, which is standard policy after an accident, and then spent the next several hours telling airline officials over and over again what had happened, which reminded me of the night of the hijacking. While we were giving our statements, someone from the airline came in and announced that José had died. Suddenly, the room seemed to become several degrees darker. I heard the voice start to explain how the doctors had done everything they could and how his injuries were just too severe to save him. His voice seemed to be drifting further and further away into a distant echo. Several of the others had started to cry, but they too sounded far away.

I don't know how long I was off in my own little world, but I snapped out of it when a police officer came into the room and instructed us not to discuss the incident from that point forward unless we were specifically asked. Apparently, the moment that José died, the Miami-Dade County Police Department began a homicide investigation, claiming that the airport was their territory. The N.T.S.B., however, claimed that the aircraft was their territory, and a power struggle promptly ensued. It took me a moment to gather my bearings and realize what was going on, and, when I did, I suddenly became very angry.

"What's going on here?" I said to the police officer. "Are we under suspicion or something?"

He responded by giving me a steely look so intense that I became a little frightened and decided to keep my mouth shut until we had a lawyer present. About five minutes later, one of the airline's attorneys came in and said that we didn't have to answer any questions asked by the police. The officer was soon summoned from the room, and the investigation was then turned over to the N.T.S.B. without further incident.

In the meantime, Doug just happened to be in Miami with a few of his friends to attend the Jets-Dolphins game, which they did every year. The accident took place the day after the game while they were out deep sea fishing. Since I was okay and didn't want him to get all worried and spoil everyone's good time, I waited until later to call him. They were planning on going out to dinner afterwards and then flying home from Fort Lauderdale later that night. I called him at the restaurant when I thought they would be finished eating. As I knew he would, he wanted to come down to the airport immediately.

"I already thought about that," I said, "and I don't want you to come. Kirsten is driving home on Wednesday from Maryland and you know that she's not the world's greatest driver, and Kelly is flying home on Wednesday. I don't want them coming home to an empty house. We might be tied up here for a few days. The N.T.S.B. said they're going to try to let us go home before Thanksgiving, but they can't guarantee it."

"I think I should be there," he said.

"No, Doug, I am okay and this is probably the best solution. Besides, none of the other crew members have their families here. I just wouldn't feel right about being the only one with a family member here."

He eventually relented, but a short time later I changed my mind and said to one of our flight service directors that I wanted to see him. She offered to drive to Fort Lauderdale and bring him back, but I quickly changed my mind again because I knew that I should be with my fellow crew members. We had lost one of our own and needed to grieve together as a crew, and Doug would have been an outsider. Later he admitted that after I spoke to him on the phone, he said, "To hell with what she wants!" and drove to Miami anyway because he felt he needed to be with me and that the girls were old enough to understand why we weren't there if they came home to an empty house. He wasn't able to find me and he tried calling my friend Patty. Patty was also flying a trip that day. American has a policy not to divulge where their flight crews are staying during a layover, and knowing that the only person who was going to give him that information was me, he finally flew back home the next day and waited.

One of the few consolations of this nightmare is that American had learned a lot since the hijacking sixteen years earlier. Back then, it was my impression that their attitude was that incidents such as this were part of your job, and that treating you with kid gloves would only make it more difficult for you to start flying again and settling back into your work routine. This time around, however, they couldn't have been any nicer in accommodating us. For instance, since our luggage was still on the plane, they offered to take us shopping for clothes and whatever else we needed. By then, I had wound up as our unofficial spokesperson and told them that the last place we wanted be right then was shopping at Macy's, so then they offered to go shopping for us. They told us to write down our sizes and everything we needed. Just before we were released to go to the hotel, our luggage was returned to us. I sometimes wonder what we would have wound up wearing if they had gone out and bought us clothes!

At the hotel, we were given an entire floor to ourselves with security guards in the hallways and airline supervisors in several of the rooms. It almost seemed like they were keeping an eye on us, so I asked one of the supervisors if all this was really necessary. He said it was, explaining that the supervisors were there just in case we needed anything and that the guards were there to keep away the press or anyone else who might bother us.

None of us wanted to go to a restaurant for dinner, so we ordered room service and ate in my room. We were all depressed and exhausted, especially now that it was starting to sink in that José was really gone. We had been so busy all afternoon answering questions and going through all the post-incident procedures that we hadn't had much time to think about what had occurred. Now that we had had a chance to talk about it amongst ourselves and think about it on our own, it just didn't seem real. Perhaps what made it so difficult to accept was that since he was a member of our crew and we were all there in the hotel together, it felt like he was there too, only in another room or something. Or, perhaps maybe it was because in a way he was there with us asking why we were all upset and trying to explain that he wasn't really gone, he was just somewhere else now.

Later that night, we watched the news on one of the local stations and became very upset at their inaccurate reporting of the story. They said that José had taken it upon himself to evacuate the plane and that he did not have the authority to do this. We immediately called the media relations department at American and complained to them about what we had just seen. They told us that they were already aware of the inaccuracies being reported by the media and that they were working on an official statement they were going to release to the press as soon as possible, but first they had to make sure that they had all the facts in order before doing so.

The next morning we met with a crisis team for a "critical incident debriefing," which was something American started doing after the hijacking. Again I was impressed with how much they had learned since then and how quickly they responded to this incident. They had set up teams of grief counselors for us to talk to if we needed them. Last time they pretty much just left us on our own to deal with the F.A.A., the F.B.I. and whoever else wanted to talk to us.

After our debriefing, we sat around the hotel most of the day waiting for the N.T.S.B. to start their individual interviews with us. At around four in the afternoon they finally started and told us that there was a good chance that they would be able to finish interviewing us that day and release us. This was good news because the next day was the day before Thanksgiving, the busiest airline travel day of the year, which might have made getting home a little bit more difficult. The last flight to New York that night was 7:00 p.m., but by 6:00 they still had four people to interview. It didn't look like we were going to make it. They did, however, agree to take two of us at a time and then take written statements from the other two. They finished interviewing us by 6:30!

The airline had limos waiting to drive us to the airport where we were met at the curb by a supervisor who had our boarding passes in hand. We were then escorted through security to the gate. Management had secured the first class cabin for the crew. They had also instructed the crew working the flight not to question us about the accident and to make sure that the other passengers left us alone. This was such a huge difference from the way the crew was treated after the hijacking. I was impressed!

After landing at JFK, we were met by several New York supervisors who informed us that they had limos waiting to take us home and employees willing to drive our cars home also. This was very considerate, but I needed to be alone with my thoughts for a little while and decided to drive myself home. Before leaving, however, one of the supervisors informed us that Jose's body was being flown to LaGuardia the next day. This is where José had started his career with American as an agent. An honor guard consisting of Jose's fellow employees was being formed to await the arrival of his coffin. I knew I wanted to be part of it. When I finally got home, Doug greeted me at the front door and said, "Jean, I can't take this anymore! I think it's time for you to quit!"

"Do you think that hasn't crossed my mind?" I said. Later he told me about his efforts to contact me and how furious he had been that I didn't want to see him down in Miami. However, he understood that I needed to be with my fellow crew members.

On Wednesday, Doug took the day off to pick up Kelly at Macarthur Airport. I was originally going to do this, but I needed to be at LaGuardia Airport. There were so many uniformed American Airlines employees waiting for Jose's plane that the terminal was a sea of blue, and I couldn't help but wonder if José actually knew all these people. Knowing him, he probably did. In fact, with all the questions he was always asking people, he probably knew them all pretty well, and they probably knew him just the same.

After Jose's plane rolled up to the gate, we were led out to the tarmac and lined up along either side of the conveyer belt ramp that was used to unload luggage from the cargo hold. Several minutes later, a pine box emerged from the belly of the plane and everyone saluted. When I saw that box moving slowly down the ramp, it hit me that this was Jose's last flight. He had died doing something that he loved, something that all of us loved, and it was heartbreaking to think that his last flight was spent in a cold dark cargo hold. For a moment, I thought I was going to lose it and start crying, but I knew I had to maintain my composure because now was not the time to express my personal grief, but to honor the ultimate sacrifice José had made in the line of duty. He deserved the same show of respect from us as police officers and firefighters and military personnel show when they lose one of their own. He gave his life attempting to save a plane full of people he thought were in danger. There is no telling what would have happened had he not been trying to open the door at that particular moment; the explosion might have taken place in a different section of the aircraft, and the outcome may have been very different.

Back inside the terminal, someone mentioned that Jose's parents were there. I wanted to talk to them, but I wasn't sure if this was the time or place to do so until one of Jose's best friends, who was also a flight attendant, came up to me and said that that his mother wanted to talk to me. She was Asian and didn't speak very much English. Jose's brother, who was a doctor out in Chicago, was also there and said he would interpret if necessary.

I was really nervous because I couldn't even begin to imagine what she was going through. It had been running through my mind about what I would say if I ever had a chance to meet her. Even so, finding the right words was still very difficult.

"Being a mother," I said to her after we had been introduced, "I know it would be important to know that my child didn't die alone. I just wanted to let you know that José was not alone out on that tarmac. We were all there with him."

She seemed to understand what I was saying, and it was heartbreaking to look into her eyes and see her pain looking back at me. After I was done speaking, she politely thanked me in English and touched my hand, and later Jose's brother told me that what I said had meant a lot to her. I talked to him for a few minutes and mentioned how José was always asking questions about every little thing. He smiled knowingly and said that José did that to get a rise out of people. He preferred interacting with others rather than just coexisting with them.

On Friday I went to the wake. I had also been planning on going to the funeral the next day, then to the memorial service that the airline was having, and finally to the wedding Doug and I had been looking forward to. When I woke up on Saturday morning, however, instead of getting dressed and ready, I went downstairs and planted myself on the couch knowing full well that I wasn't going to get up from that spot for the rest of the day.

Meanwhile, Doug was upstairs getting dressed, and when he came down and saw me still in my pajamas, he said, "Jean, I thought we had to leave in half-hour!"

"I can't do this," I said. "I can't go to a funeral in the morning and then turn around and go to a wedding and be all happy. I'm too drained to do anything."

I had already been wearing two different faces since Wednesday. It was difficult making the transition from LaGuardia Airport and then home. I was so excited to see my daughters and hear all about their college experiences. On Thanksgiving, it was difficult for me to put on an air of happiness. I did not want to project my sadness onto my family, but it was a very difficult time for me and eventually I was emotionally drained.

I didn't go back to work for three months. Besides my neck, arm, and shoulder hurting from repeatedly pulling that door handle, I was also suffering from post-traumatic stress. In all the crazy things I had been through over my career, this was the first time a co-worker had died. I had a difficult time coming to terms with it, especially since it never should have happened. Somebody should have known there was something wrong with that plane before it went up in the air, and José should still be alive today annoying us with his endless questions. He should be showing us pictures of his wedding day, and perhaps by now even showing us some baby pictures.

When I did finally go back to work, my heart wasn't in it. Every time I drove to the airport, I debated in my head whether I should quit or not. Each time Jose's voice would cut in with his questions: *Why do you want to quit? What would you do if you stopped flying? Why aren't you on that high fiber cereal diet anymore?* It was actually quite remarkable because, by questioning everything I was thinking, I was able to figure out that this decision wasn't really about me. I had been flying for twenty-five years and by now could have easily walked away having totally fulfilled my dream of being a flight attendant. It wasn't about José either, because I knew he wouldn't have wanted me to stop flying on his account.

It was about my daughters. I didn't want them to think their mom was a quitter just because something bad had happened. One of the goals Doug and I had was to put them through college without having to take out any loans. My job was allowing us to do that.

Besides, flying was what I loved to do. I knew that José understood this, because when I mentioned this to him in my head, he didn't respond by asking why.

9.

September 11

Monday, September 10, 2001 was an absolutely beautiful day. The sun was shining, it wasn't too hot or humid, and there wasn't a cloud in the sky. It was a perfect day to go to the beach, which is something I love to do in September when the summer crowds are gone and the blistering heat of August has finally given way to the cooler temperatures that signal the approach of autumn. This had always been my time of year to relax, especially when the girls were little and their summer vacations had finally come to an end, leaving me with some free time to decompress before the craziness of the holidays began. Even after they had gone off to college, I was still usually able to shift into relaxation mode and kick back a little come September. This year, however, was different.

Nine months after Jose's accident, I was still suffering from post-traumatic stress. I had been back on the job for six months and was seeing a therapist to help me work through it. Every time I thought I was making progress and things seemed to be finally getting back to normal, I would get hit with a new wave of depression. When I had first returned to work, I thought that by going through the motions and getting back into the routine of flying, my enthusiasm would eventually come back and everything would be fine. Yet, despite my desire to keep flying, I was still experiencing a feeling of dread in the days before a trip. While I truly believed that this would eventually subside until it didn't happen anymore, I didn't know how much longer I could withstand going through it every time I had to fly.

On that particular Monday, the dread became so overwhelming that I decided not to work the trip to London I was scheduled for the following morning. I didn't even feel like going through the trouble of finding someone to replace me, so I requested a vacation day instead. Moments after I had submitted the request, however, my friend Denise called and said that she had requested to work that trip when she saw that I was already signed up for it. I told her that I had just put in for a vacation day. I could tell she was disappointed because we always had fun whenever we worked together. After talking to her for a while, the idea of hanging out with her in London and going out to eat and doing a little shopping started to grow on me. I told her that I would withdraw my vacation day request. After I got off the phone with her, though, something still wasn't sitting right with me, and I sank right back into my depression.

I hoped that a day at the beach would lift my spirits a little and maybe even help me get back into my usual September groove. I gathered my things and was on my way out the door when Doug came home. He had been on jury duty for the past week and the trial had just ended. He arrived home at noon and wasn't going into his office in Manhattan until the next day. I told him that I was on my way to the beach and he decided to join me, but I was in such a lousy mood that when we got there, we wound up sitting by ourselves.

I sat in my chair staring out at the Atlantic and started thinking about TWA flight 800. I often did this whenever I went to the beach in the five years that had passed since it inexplicably exploded over the ocean not far from the very spot where I was sitting. That accident had shaken the airline industry to its core, and it is still disturbing to think that whatever really caused that plane to blow up will probably never be known, at least not by the general public.* That led me to start thinking about Jose's accident, which still upset me to the point of tears whenever I thought about it, but staring out at the ocean while I was doing so helped me start to put things in perspective. Out beyond the roar of the breakers, the ocean looked so calm and peaceful, and, despite knowing that there were things below the surface I didn't want to see, it was still very beautiful. I realized that these things would always be down there and that occasionally they were going to float up to the surface, but survival is learning how not to be pulled back down with them. There really was no other choice but to keep swimming, because if I kept treading water where I was, I would eventually tire and leave myself vulnerable and never make it back to that place out on the horizon where the sea meets the sky.

On the way home I apologized to Doug, and he took it well because he knew how difficult the past nine months had been for me. That night I fell asleep feeling a little better and thinking that maybe this time I really had finally turned a corner. Maybe that long, painful yesterday had finally come to an end, and maybe tomorrow was the new day I had been waiting for; the day when I would finally be able to start looking ahead and stop looking behind.

The next morning, I was in a much better mood. It was another beautiful day, and, after I picked up Denise, the two of us talked and laughed all the way to JFK. Our flight was not booked full and we were working with great crewmembers and looking forward to having a great trip. When we met up with the rest of the crew and signed in, everyone else seemed to be in a good mood as well. For the first time since I could remember, it actually felt good to be at work.

We had a 9:30 departure time and we started boarding the passengers at 8:45. I was working the number one position for this trip and was standing inside the aircraft door waiting to greet people as they boarded when the very first passenger to arrive mentioned to me that a plane had just crashed into the World Trade Center.

"Oh my God," I said. The passenger didn't know what kind of plane it was. My first thought was that it was probably one of those little single engine planes being flown by an amateur pilot who either didn't know what he was doing or was trying to do some foolhardy stunt like fly between the buildings or something. The passenger had assumed the same thing.

"Why do they even let these people fly?" He said to me. "He probably flies only once every six months and doesn't know what he's doing!"

A few minutes later, however, the agent came on board and pulled me aside.

"You're not going to believe this," she said. "That plane that flew into the World Trade Center was one of ours, a 767."

Flight 11.

My next thought was *what could have been so wrong with that plane that they had no choice but to fly it into the building?* It didn't even seem possible that a 767 could be that far off course to even wind up anywhere near the Manhattan skyline, never mind actually crossing that relatively miniscule area of space that the Twin Towers happened to occupy. I figured that it must have been some kind of severe mechanical malfunction where the captain totally lost control of the plane and by freak chance wound up on a collision course with the World Trade Center. As unlikely as that scenario seemed, the thought of terrorism didn't enter my mind.

There was an employee door on the jet bridge that had a window on it through which we could see the Manhattan skyline in the distance and the plume of smoke hovering over the burning tower. It was such a mind-boggling sight that it took me a few minutes to realize that at that very moment Doug was most likely near there since his office on Wall Street was pretty much right in the shadow of the towers. Although nobody yet had any idea that the building was in danger of collapsing, I suddenly realized that he might be in serious trouble and wanted get in touch with him immediately.

I tried calling his office on my cell phone, but, since all the cell phone lines in New York had jammed up right after that first plane hit, I couldn't get through. Meanwhile, the passengers continued to board the plane, and several of them sitting in first class overheard my concern and offered to try to get a call through on their cell phones. They tried calling his company's main line while I continued dialing his direct line, but none of us were successful.

Finally I said to Denise, "I don't know if I can do this flight because I need to know if Doug is okay!" She offered to call flight services and request a replacement for me and one for herself since she had driven in to work with me, but, after thinking about it for a minute, I decided that I could do the flight as long as someone kept trying to call Doug and then let me know when they were able to reach him. One of the guys who worked on the ramp was a friend of mine, so I asked him and he said he would try all day if he had to and then call the cockpit as soon he got through.

During my panic it occurred to me that I finally realized how Doug must have felt during my hijacking and then most recently with the accident in Miami. I wanted nothing more at that moment than to see for myself that he was okay, and not knowing was agonizing. It was especially frustrating to be able to see lower Manhattan with my own eyes knowing that he was down there somewhere, but not being able to help him in some way. Even during the hijacking with a gun pointed at my head I felt more in control. At that time I knew my actions were directly responsible for the fate of every person aboard that aircraft. Now all I could do was hit the redial button on my cell phone and pray that he was alright.

Denise kept telling me that I should just go home and that she would be able to find another ride, but I kept telling her that I was fine. I really wasn't, but at that point I didn't want to go home; at the airport I was at least geographically closer to Doug and there were people around me. At home, I would be by myself pulling my hair out not knowing what to do.

I was still trying to get a call through to Doug when we found out that another plane, United Airlines flight 175, had just hit the South Tower. This development brought the situation to an entirely new level. Even though it was clear by now that this was no accident, I was so worried about Doug that I didn't connect the dots and realize that these were acts of terrorism and that our country was under attack. We were watching it all happen live from the jet bridge without the benefit of CNN anchors explaining it to us. It wasn't until the captain informed us that the Pentagon had been hit by another one of our planes, flight 77, that I even realized that it was terrorism.

Doug didn't have a cell phone yet, so the only way I could try to reach him was by calling his office. I must have redialed a hundred times before I finally got through. When I did, instead of him answering the phone and assuring me that he was okay, I got his voice mail message saying he would be out indefinitely for jury duty. This was not a good sign because it meant that he probably hadn't gotten to the office yet. It seemed like every time I had ever called him at work he was at a meeting or at lunch or on the other line. This was frustrating enough under normal circumstances, but, after what I had just gone through only to reach his voice mail, I was unable to restrain my frustration.

"Damn it!" I said after the beep. "You're never there when I need to reach you! Call my cell phone and let me know that you're alright! I can't take my flight until I hear from you!"

The captain overheard me and said, "Jean, you don't have to worry about the flight right now-the airport is closed indefinitely. Everyone has been ordered to evacuate the airport immediately!

The passengers were still seated on the plane waiting to depart for London, so the captain suggested that he and I walk through the different sections of the aircraft and explain to them that their stay in the United States had been extended indefinitely and that they had to leave the airport as soon as possible. He thought that a broad P.A. announcement might create confusion, and that a calm, personal approach would have better results.

Of course, as soon as we told the first section, everyone started asking questions at once. Many of the passengers didn't live in the United States and had nowhere to stay, and just about all of them said that they had to get to London immediately. To make matters worse, we received word that the tunnels and bridges were now closed and that the subways also weren't running. While the passengers had to leave the airport, their options as to where to go were very limited.

After the captain and I had gone through the entire aircraft, we stood at the door and tried to answer any questions the passengers had as they were leaving the plane, but we really didn't know any more than what we had already told them. I felt bad knowing that many of these people had nowhere to go and were probably going to have a difficult time finding a place to stay since the hotels would be filling up fast with suddenly stranded passengers. I couldn't give them the help they needed when I didn't even know what I and the rest of the crew was going to do. So, after all the passengers had deplaned, I gathered the crew together in order to figure out what we needed to do next. This is when I found out that the South Tower had collapsed.

When I heard this, it felt like the world was coming to an end. *This can't be happening,* I thought. *This just can't be happening.* As much as I wanted to stay at the airport a short time earlier, I suddenly wanted to leave and get as far away as possible. After recovering from our initial shock at the news, we decided to head up to flight services and try to find out what we were supposed to do.

Walking through the terminal was like a bad dream—all the televisions in the waiting areas were tuned to CNN repeatedly showing a video loop of the planes flying into the buildings and the South Tower collapsing. Then we heard that another plane, United flight 93, had gone down somewhere in Pennsylvania, and that there were supposedly still more planes in the air, several of which were headed in the direction of New York City.

The flight services office was chaotic, and they gave us pretty much the same treatment that we had just given the passengers. Port Authority basically instructed everyone to leave the airport as soon as possible—passengers, airline personnel, airport employees—so that the police and the F.B.I. and whoever else would be able to inspect the airport. At this point nobody knew if this was just a first wave of attacks and if something even worse was about to happen. Whatever the case may have been, the airport didn't seem like the safest place to be, and while I was still terribly worried about Doug's fate, I was now pretty worried about my own as well.

Meanwhile, there were several stranded flight attendants who didn't live in New York and were trying to figure out what to do. After finding out that the shuttle buses to the parking lot were still running, I offered to take as many of them as I could fit into my car with Denise and me. I drove them to a hotel out in Rockville Centre where commuting flight attendants often stayed before their scheduled trips. Since it was about twenty minutes away, there would probably still be rooms available there, which at this point may not have been the case anywhere around JFK. We managed to squeeze four additional people into my car and they were all able to get rooms at the hotel. I gave each of them my home phone number in case they couldn't afford to stay too long since I had two empty bedrooms at home with the girls being away at college. The next day, one of them called to take me up on the offer, but then she called back a short time later saying she had decided to rent a car to drive back to Chicago instead. As flight attendants, we're so used to jumping on planes and arriving at our destination in a couple of hours that it seemed crazy to drive fifteen hours just to get to Chicago, which is about the same amount of time it would take to fly all the way to Tokyo!

After dropping Denise off at her house, I hurried back home and found I had many messages on the answering machine. I hit the play button and skipped through them trying to find one from Doug, but there wasn't one. After I had gotten through the last message, the phone rang and I picked it up anxiously hoping it was him, but it was my brother, who was a Suffolk County narcotics detective at the time, calling to make sure that I was okay. It was about three in the afternoon by now and I told him how worried I was that I hadn't heard from Doug yet. While I was telling him this, I started to cry. He was able to calm me down by reminding me that the subways weren't running and that the only way out of Manhattan right now was by foot, so it was probably going to take him a while to get home.

"I'm sure he's fine," he said. "Let's just give him until six. I don't know if I'll be able to do anything, but, if you haven't heard from him by then, I'll see if I can get in touch with someone."

Just then Doug's Jeep pulled into the driveway, so I excitedly told my brother that he was home and hurried outside. He was covered from head to toe in soot and grime, but I didn't care and gave him a big hug and a kiss anyway. As we were heading into the house, he said that before we started telling each other about our day, he was going to take a shower and asked that I have a beer waiting for him on the front porch.

When Doug had climbed up the stairs of the subway station near his office that morning, the sky was raining paper, which at first made him think there was a ticker tape parade going on. Having been on jury duty on Long Island for more than a week, he had no idea what the parade could have been for and tried to figure it out as he made his way to the office. Before he got there, however, he overheard people on the street saying that a plane had crashed into the North Tower. He hurried up to his office and started asking around if anyone knew what airline it was. Nobody knew as of yet, and it was right about then that the second plane hit the South Tower. Being so close to the World Trade Center, everyone in the office was obviously scared out of their minds, but perhaps no one more than Doug. He knew that I was flying that morning, and, with my track record, he began to fear the worst. He asked his secretary to try and find out what airline the planes were while he checked his voice mail to see if I or anyone else who might have known something left him a message.

Since he had been out of the office for so long, his box was flooded with messages, and it took him a while to get through them. Just as he hit the button to hear my message, his secretary popped her head in the door.

"Doug, I don't know how to tell you this," she said, "but that first plane was American Airlines."

Suddenly my voice exploded through the earpiece ordering him to call me right away or else I wouldn't be able to take my flight.

"She's fine," he said with a laugh of relief. "She is absolutely fine."

Later he told me that if my message hadn't started playing when it did, he probably would have passed out. He then tried to call me back on my cell, but he wasn't able to get a line out either. A short time later, Manhattan went into lockdown mode, and the only way to get anywhere was on foot, so Doug and tens of thousands of others who worked in lower Manhattan set out for the Brooklyn Bridge. Fortunately, he had gotten far enough away not to be hurt when the first tower collapsed, but he wasn't spared from being completely covered with dust and soot. After crossing the bridge into Brooklyn, he had to walk about seven miles to get to a Long Island Rail Road station. While the trains weren't running into Penn Station, they had resumed service east of Manhattan, so he was able to catch one that took him back home.

The weather had been absolutely beautiful that September, and every evening after dinner we had gone for a walk. After Doug had finished telling me about his day, I smiled at him and said, "So, does that mean we're not going walking tonight?"

"I'm not going anywhere but to the fridge to get another beer," he said.

Despite what a tragic day it had been, I felt relieved more than anything because Doug was okay. In the following weeks, though, with time to think about what had occurred as it took about a month for the airlines to resume normal flight schedules, I was once again faced with the question as to whether or not I should continue flying. Oddly enough, unlike Jose's accident, which had nearly broken my spirit, the attacks of September 11 emboldened me and strengthened my desire to keep flying. As a New Yorker and as an American, I could not allow terrorists to make this decision for me. As a mother, I wasn't going to set a bad example for my daughters by letting terrorism rule my life. Although I didn't know any of the American Airlines employees who died that day, I felt their loss very deeply. It was important to me to keep flying in their honor. They probably loved flying just as much as I did, and I didn't want to let their murderers instill a fear that would jeopardize our profession. If flight attendants started quitting because of what these savages had done, then they would have succeeded in their purpose. I felt an obligation to do my part to show that we had not been defeated, and that their mission of hatred was not successful.

Of course, now that terrorists were using commercial airliners as weapons, I was more than a bit nervous when I did go back to work. Despite all the security upgrades implemented after the attacks that probably made flying safer than it had been at any point in my career, the scary part was the realization that there were people in this world who would willingly give up their lives to kill as many of us as they could and how naive we were not to perceive this threat. It was also sad to think that we could no longer trust anyone who boarded our planes. Every single passenger had to be regarded as a potential threat, and even the slightest disturbance that occurred during the course of a flight had to be treated as a life-threatening situation. It is hard to believe that when I first started flying, most people thought of flight attendants as pretty faces whose main purpose was to make the experience of flying as pleasant as possible for passengers. Now here we were suddenly being perceived as the first line of defense in our nation's skyways and ready to pounce on anyone who made one false move!

10.

Flight 587

In early November, a rumor started going around that on September 11, there were three suspected terrorists aboard our 8:30 flight to London out of JFK. My friend Debbie was working that flight, which was scheduled to depart from the gate directly across from where my 9:30 London flight was departing that morning. Shortly after Debbie's flight pulled away from the gate, however, the captain reported a mechanical problem with the aircraft and headed back to the terminal. Before the mechanics had a chance to look at the aircraft, the first of the hijacked planes crashed into the World Trade Center. A short time later all flights were cancelled, so Debbie never left the ground that day.

Although the rumor about the terrorists was never officially confirmed, it wasn't denied either. And, since the four planes that went down that morning had departure times of 7:59, 8:14, 8:20, and 8:42, it seems reasonable to believe that an 8:30 flight to London could have been another mark for the terrorists, especially since it was a big Boeing 777 with a full tank of gas.

On the same morning I heard the rumor, I ran into Debbie at JFK while she was signing in for a flight.

"Debbie," I said. "I just heard that your London flight had three terrorists on it!"

"I heard that too," she said. "I just told [my husband] Steve that I wasn't picking up overtime anymore. Jean, after all you've been through, why do you still do it?"

Over the past year I had certainly thought about retiring early because of the emotional toll my experiences had taken on me, but fear of death was not really a factor in that decision. In the days and weeks following September 11, I realized that you can't just hide in your house watching CNN every waking hour waiting for the next bad thing to happen. All those innocent people who died that day were simply going about their everyday lives and had no control over how they met their end. No one does. I believe that when your number's up, your number is up, and there really isn't anything you can do about it. There didn't seem to be much sense in worrying about the inevitable.

I think Debbie also realized this after the initial shock of hearing that terrorists may have been on her plane had worn off because she didn't even bring it up when I saw her a week later. It had now been two months and a day since 9/11, and things were slowly but surely starting to return to normal. Debbie and I were on the employee bus at JFK that was taking us from the parking lot to the terminal with several of the other crew members who were scheduled to work flight 587 with Debbie to Santo Domingo, a route I had flown many times myself. That morning, I was working a flight to St. Maarten scheduled to depart a few minutes before theirs.

It was a cold and cloudy morning, the first time that fall that I had to wear my uniform coat. I was sitting next to Debbie on the bus and she was telling me how she had to cancel the doctor's appointment she had in the city that day. Her request for a personal vacation day had been denied. She was stuck working the Santo Domingo flight. I told her that she was lucky in a way because the president was in town, and that always caused a major traffic headache. Then we started chit-chatting about our kids. She was telling me how her son was doing at college down in Daytona and I was telling her how Kelly was doing at school in Orlando. Having kids the same age was one of the reasons we became such good friends. We were always talking about them and comparing notes and sharing our joys and sorrows with each other. In the days following Jose's accident, I often thought that talking to Debbie was doing me more good than seeing a therapist because I knew she understood what I was going through more than someone who sat in a leather chair all day listening to the problems of strangers with whom they had nothing in common.

After signing in for my flight at the operations office, I ran into Barbara who was scheduled to work flight 587 with Debbie. We started talking in front of the elevator when Debbie came by and said she was heading downstairs to the gate. She had one foot in the elevator when I reminded her about our luncheon on that upcoming Wednesday. She said she was looking forward to it and would see me there as the elevator doors slid shut. Flight attendants who live on Long Island try to get together once a month for lunch. These luncheons first started when I was pregnant in 1980 with Kirsten. At that time flight attendants were removed from flight status when you were pregnant. One day a few months into my pregnancy I invited a few of my flight attendant friends over for lunch. We had so much fun that we continued getting together once a month at each others homes until our children started school. After that we scheduled our luncheons at various restaurants on Long Island.

I continued talking to Barbara, who had just returned to work after having been out on a leave of absence. That month, she had been flying mostly to Paris, which was her favorite route .Paris is where Barbara and her husband had gotten married. The Santo Domingo flight was an extra trip she picked up at the last minute. She hadn't worked this flight very often, so I told her to get ready for some long delays. One of the other flight attendants working 587, Joe, overheard me telling Barbara about this and said, "Yeah, lucky us," before disappearing into the elevator. Finally I said that I had to go since I was supposed to be down at the gate for my own flight in a few minutes. Barbara said goodbye and that she would see me at lunch on Wednesday.

I was also looking forward to lunch on Wednesday. I love the fall and was looking forward to the upcoming holiday season. The passenger load for my flight was light, and the trip was a turnaround, which meant that I would be home later that night. A couple of hours into the flight everything seemed to be going smoothly until the captain called me up to the cockpit.

When I got there, the captain and two first officers simultaneously turned their heads towards me and just kind of stared. I knew something was going on. There was a long moment of silence before the captain finally said that they had something to tell me.

"What is it?" I said with a knot in my stomach. The way they were looking at me was so strange. "We just lost 587," he said.

"Lost?" I said. "What do you mean *lost*? You mean it's no longer on the radar?"

He looked at the other two for a moment before looking up at me.

"It crashed, Jean."

It took a few seconds for my mind to comprehend what he had said.

"What?"

"587 went down a few minutes after it took off. Nobody knows what happened yet, so we've been put on high alert."

"What does that mean?"

"Well, since we're in the air, it doesn't really mean anything to us now. At this point, whatever's going to happen-if we have a bomb on board or something—is going to happen. We're way over water right now and they're not re-routing us, so we're proceeding to St. Maarten as scheduled. Just keep your eyes and ears open for anything suspicious."

I was in a daze. I had heard everything the captain said, but the words just weren't registering.

"Jean," he said, "I don't think you should tell the rest of the crew about 587 until we're on the ground."

"I can't NOT tell the crew!" I said, my eyes now welling with tears as I finally started to realize the significance of what had happened.

"Alright," he said. "Just don't let the passengers know."

"No," I said. "I won't let the passengers know."

After leaving the cockpit, I was overcome by this tremendous fear that put my "when your numbers up" theory to the ultimate test. I knew that the captain was right. If there was a bomb on board (which was at first what most of us thought had happened to 587), there was nothing we could do about it. So, according to the theory, I shouldn't have been worried. Yet, I quickly realized that this only works when there isn't a specific, perceived threat staring you in the face, such as the possibility that there is a bomb on your aircraft that could go off at any second. Similar to the hijacking after we had landed in Cuba and I thought the hijacker was about to make good on his vow to kill both the captain and myself, I thought that I was about to die. As scared as I was, however, I knew that I had to compose myself immediately in order to tell the rest of the crew about the crash. It turned out to be one of the most difficult things I've ever had to do as a flight attendant.

I decided that it would be better to tell them one at a time, so I first asked Donna to step back into the galley. This was the first time I had ever flown with Donna, so I really didn't know her too well and was unaware that she had been working with Debbie on the 8:30 London flight on September 11. Since she lived in New Jersey and had no way of getting home that day with the bridges and tunnels being closed, she actually spent the night at Debbie's house on Long Island. After telling her that 587 had crashed, she started crying hysterically and kept saying, "Oh my God, Debbie was on that flight! Oh my God!"

"Donna," I said, placing my hands on her shoulders, "Debbie was my friend too and I'm really upset about it, but you've got to get a grip here. We don't want the passengers to know about the crash because they might start to panic. Why don't you just stay here in the galley and not come out until you've calmed down."

A couple of the other flight attendants heard Donna crying and came back to see what was wrong, so at that point I knew it was no use trying to tell everyone individually. After gathering the rest of the crewmembers in the galley, I gave them the news, and they all just stood there in shock. Somebody asked what had caused the crash and I said that I didn't know, but that we couldn't just assume that it was terrorism. Saying this actually helped calm my own nerves because up until I said this, with September 11 still so fresh in our minds, I hadn't yet really considered the possibility that it wasn't terrorism.

"We have to keep our emotions in check and finish this flight," I said. "There will be time to grieve later, but right now we can't let the passengers get wind of this and think this is another 9/11."

As difficult as it was, our sense of duty prevailed and we managed to shift our focus back to our jobs. With our minds on the crash and on the possibility that something might happen on our own flight, the crew hardly said a word as there really didn't seem to be anything else to talk about. This silence only added to the tension we were already feeling until we finally touched down safely in St. Maarten a couple of hours later.

After the passengers had deplaned, we hurried over to the operations office to check the crew list for 587 and to see if CNN had any more information as to the cause of the crash. By the time we got there, though, the list had already been removed from the computer system, which is done immediately after an accident to protect the privacy of the family members. After making a couple of phone calls, however, we were able to get the names of the crew members.

I was worried that another good friend of mine might have been on that flight as well since she had been flying with Debbie all month, but I didn't see her name on the list. While I was relieved that her name wasn't on there, seeing all those other names was absolutely heartbreaking. I knew just about all of them, and, having spoken to Debbie and Barbara only a few hours earlier, it was too soon for my mind to accept that they were really gone. First it was Jose's accident, then September 11, and now this, all in less than a year (the one year anniversary of Jose's accident was eight days after the crash of 587). It was just too much. As strong as I knew I was, I also knew there was a limit, and that whenever the reality of this tragedy did finally sink in, it was surely going to take me well beyond mine.

At the same time, I also knew that I had at least one more flight ahead of me. When the captain came in and saw me crying, he came over and put his arm around my shoulder.

"Jean," he said, "if you and the rest of the crew don't want to go home today, we can lay over."

I knew he only suggested it because he thought we might be too upset to go right back up in the air and work, but I couldn't help thinking, *what are we going to do, swim home?* Since we had to go home sooner or later, sooner was preferable because I would have rather grieved at home than in a hotel room in St. Maarten. I told him that I was ready to work the flight, but suggested that he ask the rest of the crew what they wanted to do before making any decisions. He agreed and gathered the others for a briefing. Despite knowing how difficult this flight would be, we unanimously decided to work the scheduled turnaround flight to JFK. We all wanted to get home as soon as possible and begin what was to be yet another round of grieving and recovery. After the decision was made, the captain reminded us that in working this flight we had a responsibility to our passengers, and that even though we were all very upset about what had happened, we absolutely could not let our emotions interfere with our duty.

Fortunately, we had another light load back to New York, and many of the passengers expressed their condolences for the loss of our coworkers since they knew about the crash from watching CNN in the St. Maarten terminal. They were very considerate and pretty much left us alone all the way back to New York, which was helpful, but it was still a long, quiet flight that didn't seem like it was ever going to end.

When we finally arrived back at JFK, we were greeted at the gate by several flight service directors and escorted upstairs to one of the conference rooms, where the chaplain who had hosted many of the airline's grief counseling sessions after September 11 was talking to some of the flight crews who had worked that day and arrived at JFK after the crash. When we entered the room, he had us sit down and expressed how sorry he was about this latest tragedy and then started talking about the importance of grieving properly and how there was a reason why this happened that we may not yet understand.

"I have noticed that flight attendants have a camaraderie similar to firefighters and police officers," he said. "It is good that you have each other during times like these. It promotes a healthy atmosphere for grieving and makes the process of acceptance a little less strenuous. A lot of times when tragedy strikes, people turn to outside sources like drugs or alcohol to help them cope, but that only provides temporary relief from pain and only prolongs the process of healing."

"Then you don't know flight attendants very well, because we definitely do alcohol!" I said, trying to lighten the somber atmosphere in the room with my dry sense of humor. As soon as I said it, however, I knew that I should have kept my mouth shut, a realization that was confirmed by the silence that followed and the glare that the chaplain was giving me. But I couldn't help it. I had been keeping my anguish in check all day, and it was becoming increasingly more difficult to continue doing so.

A little while later, the base manager came in and informed me that Don Carty wanted to see me. Don Carty was the C.E.O. of American Airlines at the time and had flown in from Dallas as soon as he heard about the crash. I had met him once before after José died, and he seemed like a nice man, but I didn't think this was a good time to talk to him. I was worried that, having held in my anguish for this long, I was going to lose it in front of him. So I said to the manager, "I'm in the middle of this grieving session right now," and she left. A couple of minutes later, however, she came back and asked once more, and again I said no. Perhaps I was in such a state that I wasn't fully aware that I was refusing the C.E.O. of the entire company, and the chaplain's words were providing comfort, so I didn't want to leave. Several minutes later, however, Don himself came in and asked me for a word, so I finally relented and followed him down the hall into a vacant conference room.

"Jean," he said, taking a seat across the table from me. "I just wanted to personally apologize for this tragedy and pass along my condolences. My heart aches for the loss of your colleagues."

"Thank you," I said.

"I know you've been through one thing after another, and you have my full respect and admiration for sticking with us. Jean-is there anything I can do for you?"

"Actually, there is-you can make this airline a whole lot safer!"

He said he would do everything in his power to make that happen and asked me to let him know if there was anything else he could do. Afterwards, I realized that for him to think of *my* well-being amid all the family members he still had to address, as well as the media and the board of directors and whoever else who was waiting to talk to him, was actually pretty extraordinary. Even so, when I was driving home later that night, I couldn't help thinking that my career as a flight attendant was now probably over.

Upon our arrival in St. Maarten earlier in the day, I had called Doug to let him know that I was okay. In doing so, I thought that he would then be able to just tell anyone who called checking to see if I had been on 587 that I was fine, and that would be the end of that. When I finally got back home that night, however, he said that I needed to call the girls right away. They had apparently been very upset after finding out about the crash because they thought I might have been on that plane, and, although Doug told them that I was okay, they still instructed him to have me call them the moment I got home.

Having been up since five that morning and going through a yet another hellish day at the office, I was exhausted and didn't really feel like making phone calls. But I remembered how I felt waiting to hear from Doug on September 11 and I knew it was important that they hear directly from me that I was okay, so I made the calls. They both sounded fine now that they had had a chance to calm down, and they understood that I was exhausted, so they didn't keep me on the phone for too long. Afterwards, Doug told me about the calls they had made to him at work after each of them found out about the crash.

Kirsten was student teaching at the time and had been out all day, so she didn't find out about the crash until she got back to her apartment. Her roommate was watching CNN when she came in and asked, "Hey, Kir, doesn't your mom work for American?"

Kirsten said that I did, and, upon being told about the crash and that it was a flight from JFK to Santo Domingo, she began to panic because she knew I was flying that day and that I often worked the Santo Domingo route. She called Doug at work and he assured her that I was on the St. Maarten flight and that I was fine, and although he was able to calm her down, she was still very upset afterwards. She more than anyone had wanted me to quit after September 11, and this only strengthened her desire for me to do so. She didn't think she would be able to withstand another emotional roller coaster ride like the ones she had already been through.

Kelly had a similar reaction when she found about the crash, which at that time surprised me. Up until then, Kelly and I had the usual mother/daughter relationship during her high school years. She had been the rebellious teenager with the attitude and all the arguments that go along with it. Even though it was pretty much just typical teenage stuff that so many mothers and daughters go through, it had driven a wedge between us that was still there after she left home to attend college. She had been an independent child since the moment she was born. I used tell her that I felt at eighteen she would just leave home and we would never hear from her again. I jokingly told her she had to promise to at least call on my birthday and all the holidays. She responded with "well, okay, but it will probably have to be collect!"

When news broke of the crash, Kelly had been watching CNN, as she had every morning since her boyfriend at the time was in the Air Force. When CNN said that it was an American Airlines flight from JFK to Santo Domingo, she became hysterical and immediately called Doug. This was several hours before Kirsten had called, and although Doug hadn't yet heard about the crash, he was able to calm her down somewhat by telling her that he was pretty sure that I was flying to St. Maarten that day. He said that he would check with the airline just to be sure. Before doing so, however, he called my sister-in-law, Lori, who is Kelly's godmother and put her on a three way call with Kelly. Lori continued to calm Kelly down while Doug placed a call to my girlfriend Patty in Florida. Patty's daughter, Crystal, was attending the same college as Kelly. Doug wanted Crystal to be with Kelly just in case he was incorrect about which flight I was working. He then called American and was able to confirm that I was on the St. Maarten flight. Kelly was now twenty. With all the love and concern she showed that day, I knew those rebellious teenage years were gone!

The next morning, I called Debbie's husband Steve. I had never met Steve, but Debbie had told me so much about him that I felt like I already knew him. He was a base manager for United Airlines, so Debbie and I used to have some pretty lively discussions whenever union negotiations started up. With her husband being on the other side, she often looked at things from management's point of view.

Whoever answered the phone informed me that Steve wasn't taking any calls. When he heard it was me, however, he got on the phone and he said, "You're one of the few people I'm willing to talk to right now."

"But you don't even know me!" I said.

"Yes, but Debbie talks about you a lot, so I know a lot about you."

"Steve, I've been getting a lot of calls from other flight attendants who want to come over, but we wouldn't come unless you wanted us to."

"Actually, I think I'd like that. Come on over."

Within minutes, there were about twenty flight attendants who wanted to go, but one of the questions that kept coming up was whether or not we should wear our uniforms. Because Debbie had died in the line of duty, I thought it would be appropriate if we did, so I told everyone that I was going to wear mine, but that the decision was up to them. As it turned out, just about everyone else did show up in uniform.

When I got to the house, there was a woman standing out front who looked very much like Debbie. I introduced myself and said, "You must be Debbie's sister."

"No, I'm actually Debbie's best friend," she said. "I'm also a flight attendant."

I had never met this woman before and it seemed sort of surreal because she looked so much like Debbie. She was waiting for someone and stayed outside while I went into the house, where Debbie's family was gathered and where I finally got to meet Steve. After talking to him for only a couple of minutes, I could tell what a great guy he was, which made it even more heartbreaking that we had to meet under these circumstances.

"You know, Steve," I said, "Debbie talked about you all the time, but you're not anything like what I pictured you to be."

"Is that good or bad?" he asked.

"It's good, it's good. I just think it's funny that we hear all the stories about each other's husbands and relatives and you form a picture in your mind about what they're like. When you finally do get to meet them, they don't turn out to be anything like you had imagined!"

Our conversation was interrupted when Steve got a call from someone who said that they needed some of Debbie's DNA to identify her remains and that he would need to give them a hairbrush or a toothbrush or something. Hearing this was very upsetting. Until then, I was remembering Debbie as she was when she was still alive and now someone was using the word "remains." Steve, however, was holding up incredibly well and said that he would get right on it. He also was making arrangements for his son and Debbie's mother to be picked up at the airport and playing host to everyone showing up at the house. It was almost as if he was there for them rather than the other way around. It was truly heartbreaking to watch him because it was obvious that it hadn't really sunk in yet that Debbie was gone, and, when it did, it was probably going to hit him pretty hard.

I stayed for a couple of hours until several of the other flight attendants said they were heading over to Barbara's house. When I was saying good-bye to Steve, he said, "You know, Jean, when I got off the phone with you earlier I said to myself, *I hope they don't show up wearing their uniforms.* I really thought that would bother me. But now I'm glad you did because I know that was an important part of Debbie's life. I just wanted to thank you for doing it."

Barbara and her husband John lived in the oceanfront community of Point Lookout in this gorgeous house that Barbara often jokingly referred to as "The House That'll Never get Done." They had been in the process of remodeling, but, whenever they finished part of it, John decided that he didn't like it and had it done all over again. Every month she'd bring new pictures of the house to work, and soon it became a running joke. Even unfinished, though, it was still a spectacular home. She wasn't sure at first if she would like living in Point Lookout since it was so much different than her native Buffalo, but, after she and John moved there, she fell in love with it.

There were several family members gathered at the house, but John wasn't there. Shortly after hearing the news, he left the house and began the fifteen mile walk to the crash site in Belle Harbor. I couldn't even begin to imagine what he was going through. I knew they were happily married and that they were both madly in love with each other. Since they didn't have any children, losing Barbara was like losing everything he had. I still think about her every time I fly to Paris, and what a sweet, bubbly, lovable person she was.

The next day was supposed to be our luncheon, which I assumed had been cancelled, so I hadn't really given the luncheon much thought. That morning I received a call from Merryl, the coordinator of our monthly luncheons. She said that she had been receiving a lot of calls from flight attendants who still wanted to meet for lunch.

"You're kidding," I said.

"I think everyone just wants to be together," she said.

We decided to go ahead with our original plans to meet at the Macaroni Grill in Westbury. We would leave two empty chairs for Debbie and Barbara since they were supposed to join us. Out of fifteen or so regulars, usually between six and ten showed up for the monthly luncheon since everybody had different schedules. This time, however, people who had never even been to one before started showing up. The staff was very accommodating as they kept adding more tables and chairs. Of course, increasing the supply of wine was a necessity also. Then, to my utter surprise, who walks in but my friend, the chaplain from the grieving session at the airport!

I invited him to pull up a chair and told him how surprised I was to see him there. He said he had been over at JFK hosting a grieving session when word got out about our luncheon.

"I decided to come just in case anyone needed me," he said.

"We appreciate that, chaplain," I said. "What's your preference- red or white?"

"White, please," he said, and I couldn't help but crack a smile as I poured him a glass.

"You see?" I said. "I told you flight attendants did alcohol!"

He laughed, and the tension between us was broken. After talking to him for a little while, I began to realize that, having spent so much time with flight attendants over the last couple of months, he really was beginning to understand what we were like. He knew that all we really needed was each other, because at 35,000 feet, that's all we had.

I attended every one of the funerals for the flight attendants of 587 except for two. The memorial service for Debbie was right before Thanksgiving. We had to wait outside before it started because the children were using the church for their Thanksgiving pageant, which was running a little late. A lone bagpiper played the entire time we were out there and it was terribly sad, but also very beautiful. Debbie's was the first of the funerals and after that it was one right after the other. There was also a huge memorial service held at St. Agnes Church in Rockville Centre where different employees from the airline got up and said something about each of the flight attendants from 587. Debbie's best friend was asked to say something about Debbie, but she didn't think she would be able to do it. She called and asked me if I wanted to do it instead. I would have, but I thought that it would be more appropriate for her to do it since she was Debbie's best friend. I managed to convince her to at least think about it, and she said she would if I first looked at what she had written. A couple of days later I received a photocopy of it in the mail, and I called her back as soon as I had finished reading it.

"Are you sure you don't want to read this?" I said. "Because it is absolutely beautiful!"

"I don't know if I can," she said.

"You should at least try, because this is going to be your last chance to do this. If you can't get through it, then I'll jump right in and finish it for you."

She did manage to get through it and did a wonderful job. More than a few tears were shed while she was up there. All the speeches were beautiful, as was the service, and afterwards we finally started to feel a little closure.

The holidays were rough. I helped Merryl plan our big annual holiday luncheon, which was about twice as large as usual since this was the first holiday season after September 11 and flight 587. A lot of people who had lost someone close to them felt a need to be together. Debbie's husband Steve and Barbara's husband John were among those who joined us. I think it was good for them to be around so many people who cared about their wives and for them to spend some time with each other. I also had my own family gatherings to worry about. With all the shopping and cooking and baking and everything else I was busy doing, I hardly had a spare moment to think about whether or not I wanted to go back to work.

After the holidays, however, I had all the free time in the world to think about it. I was on an indefinite leave of absence. It was important to me to take as much time off as I needed before going back, but I honestly didn't think that was going to happen. No longer was it a matter of setting an example for my daughters, because they had already learned the lessons I had to teach them about not giving up when things got rough, particularly after Jose's accident and September 11. Additionally, Doug had said that we could probably get by without having to take out any student loans for the girls even if I didn't go back. In fact, just about everyone I was close to told me that maybe I should seriously consider retiring, and I knew they were right.

Going back was now merely a question of my desire to continue flying. Even though whatever desire I had left to do so had seemingly gone down with flight 587, I thought I should keep the door open, just in case. In the meantime, I needed to find out what my life would be like without flying. It had been over twenty-five years since I had been to that place, and I had absolutely no idea what would be there now.

But I had to look. That was the only place I was going to find the answer.

II.

Born to Fly

As the days turned into weeks and the weeks turned into months, I kept myself busy doing a whole lot of nothing while drifting aimlessly towards the dawn of middle age. I hadn't even seen this stage of my life coming while I was still flying, and I certainly didn't want to think of myself as *middle-aged*. A word like *retirement* has a way of conjuring up that term. Fortunately I was still a long way from receiving Social Security checks, and I still felt young and had plenty of energy left to embark on a new career. What that new career would be, however, I had absolutely no idea.

In the meantime, I tried not to think about flying. I succeeded for the most part, but, like most things you consciously try to ignore, I always knew it was there. One thing that kept popping in my head was that, having been a flight attendant since I was twenty-two, flying was the connection to my youth. I was worried that by severing that tie, I would instantly transform into an old age. I was far from ready for that, but, if I didn't find something else to do, I was afraid that it just might happen.

That April I turned fifty, and for my birthday Doug and I went on a cruise. It left from Fort Lauderdale with stops in Cozumel, then Jamaica, and finally to Grand Cayman. It was a wonderful trip, and I had plenty of time to plant myself in a deck chair and stare out at the sea. In doing so, I finally allowed myself to think about flying again, which I hadn't done in several months.

I had been avoiding it because I thought Jose's accident, September 11, and flight 587 would immediately come to my mind and I was emotionally drained from thinking about these things so much already. But that didn't really happen. What actually came to mind was the very first time I had considered quitting back in 1979 after the crash of flight 191 in Chicago. At the time, I had been flying for nearly five years without incident, and, not being a mother yet back then, I was more of a free-spirit and pretty much fearless. I was en route to San Juan when it happened and was flying on a DC-10, the same model of plane that had crashed and the same model that was often used on the trips I was assigned to.

After the crash, the F.A.A. immediately grounded all DC-10s for inspection, and, with so many planes suddenly taken out of service, the entire airline industry went into disarray. Passengers and crews became stranded all over the world. I ended up being stuck in San Juan for five days. Crew scheduling was still being done with pencil and paper at this time and not by computers. It didn't take long before they began to lose track of where everyone was. We all had to check in with them every day to see if we had a flight back home. It was a total mess, but we made the best of it. There were two whole floors of flight attendants at the hotel where we were staying, so there was always something fun going on. After five days of sightseeing, going out to dinner, lying by the pool, and partying in our rooms, however, I was relieved at finally being assigned to work a 707 back to New York. I was absolutely exhausted and ready to go back home.

The DC-10s were grounded for several months before the F.A.A. finally declared them airworthy. I was on reserve during the month they were put back into service. One night at around two in the morning, crew scheduling called to tell me that I had been assigned to work the 7:00 AM flight to San Juan the next morning, which had always been a DC-10 flight.

"Is it a DC-10?" I asked the scheduler on the other end.

"Yes," he said.

"Well, gee, do you think you can find someone else?"

"Do you think I'd be calling you at two in the morning if I could find someone else?"

It was to be the first DC-10 flight since the crash in Chicago, which was reason enough to be nervous. I had known that the DC-10s were eventually going to be put back in service and that I would be working them again, but I had not anticipated working the first one to go back in the air following the crash. It would have been a lot easier if a few flights had landed safely before then so I could at least use those as assurances that everything was going to be fine. There seemed to be no time in between the flight they wanted me to work in the morning and what still remains one of the worst disasters in the history of commercial aviation.

Gone suddenly was the safe, carefree little world I had been flying around in for the past five years in my pretty Bill Blass uniforms. I was now being forced to take a bold step into the polyester era with the realization that this job was not only lacking in glamour, it was also dangerous! I had never been afraid to fly before-not when I was seven, and not when I was twenty-seven-but now, for the first time in my life, I was nervous about boarding an aircraft.

"Guess what?" I said to Doug after hanging up the phone. "I'm flying the first DC-10 back in the air! What luck!"

"You shouldn't be too worried," he said. "They wouldn't be putting them back in the air unless they were safe."

"That's easy for you to say-I noticed that you aren't flying on one tomorrow! Would you care to join me?"

"I don't think so," he said and went back to sleep.

Sometimes I wonder if I would have stepped on that plane the next morning if we had had children at the time. After Kirsten was born, my perspective on life changed so drastically that I wasn't sure if I should even continue flying. I was frightened by the thought of her growing up without a mother. While I was still on maternity leave, Doug and I drew up wills stating who Kirsten's legal guardian would be if something were to happen to us. The job went from being a fun way to make a living to a very serious and even risky occupation. I especially didn't like having to spend any extra time away from home. Before then I kind of liked when things didn't go according to schedule. It was exciting to have unexpected layovers in all these different cities, but all that changed once the kids came along.

I was still about a year away from that, however, so, despite being nervous, I boarded that plane the next morning without hesitation. I felt a little better when I saw that some of the airline's most experienced pilots had been assigned to work that flight. In addition to the captain, first officer, and flight engineer, there would also be two chief pilots and two F.A.A. officials squeezed into the cockpit with them. With seven of the most experienced people in the airline industry up there, what could possibly go wrong?

About forty-five minutes before landing in San Juan, the captain called the number one flight attendant to the cockpit. A few minutes later she came back out and informed us that we had to prepare for an emergency landing because the cockpit wasn't sure if they had any landing gear.

"Are you kidding me?" I said. "All those experts up there and they can't even figure out if we have any landing gear?"

Despite how serious this sounds, it actually isn't all that uncommon an occurrence—it usually only turns out to be a blown bulb on the instrument panel and the landing gear is working just fine. On this particular morning the crew and passengers were already on edge from all the media attention this flight received. This being the first DC-10 returned to flight status, the passengers started to panic after the announcement was made that we would be following emergency landing procedures. We explained that this was just a precaution and that everything was probably fine, but that didn't do much to calm their nerves. Rosary beads came out, people started praying and crying and saying "I love you!" to one another. Even the flight attendants were nervous once we were buckled into our jump seats after completing our tasks and the captain had made the "prepare for landing" announcement.

As the plane descended towards the runway, I remember thinking, *Okay, this is it. Maybe we have landing gear, maybe we don't. Maybe we'll do a belly landing and everything will be fine, or maybe it won't. Whatever is about to happen, there isn't a thing I can do about it.* Out the window I could see that we were about to land and from that point to when we actually touched down seemed like an eternity. But it was a perfect landing, and it did turn out to be a five cent light bulb that caused all the worry.

Later I called Doug and said, "*They wouldn't put them back in the air unless they were safe,* huh? Well, let me tell you what I just went through!"

Little did I realize at the time how significant this flight would be to the rest of my career. It set a precedent for all the times I thought about quitting in the future whenever something big happened in my personal life or in the industry, such as my daughters being born, the hijacking, the bombing of Pan Am flight 103, TWA flight 800, Jose's accident, September 11, and everything else in between. No matter what had happened, I always went back.

But why did I keep going back?

I pondered this question one afternoon while sitting on the deck overlooking the Caribbean after the ship had departed from Cozumel. Having spent the past several months cooped up at home, it felt good to be back out in the world again, especially to an area where I had flown so many times over my career. Since I was feeling good and that so far I hadn't been flooded with dark thoughts while thinking about flying, I allowed myself to probe a little deeper.

Time and time again I had been asked why I kept going back, and I always had an answer ready. This question was usually asked during conversations I would be having with someone about the incidents that have happened over my career. My answer usually corresponded to the context of that conversation. I would say something like, *Oh, I'm not afraid. I figure that when your number's up, your number's up, so there's no use in worrying about it.* It occurred to me now, however, that this had not really answered the question. Not being afraid of doing something is not a reason to continue doing it.

The answer is that I love to fly. I've loved it since I was seven years old, and I truly feel that this is what I was born to do. Over the years, this love of flying has sometimes been covered by the emotional baggage left behind by some of the things that have happened, but that love was still there and hadn't been altered. Since it was still there, and I thought I may have reached the point where I had moved on from the recent tragedies, what, if anything, was preventing me from going back?

I began to consider the possibility that I might be trying to avoid future tragedy. Then I realized that this didn't make sense because not flying wasn't going to make something that happens less tragic. It wasn't so much my own death I was afraid of, and, God forbid, if another plane did go down with people on it whom I knew, how would that be any less painful if I wasn't flying?

Then I started to think that maybe it was the reminders of past tragedies that I was trying to avoid. Maybe I thought that driving to the airport would make me think about this bad thing or that bad thing, or that in the middle of a flight I might suddenly be seized by some overwhelming grief that would prevent me from doing my job. But why? Why did I think all my memory associations with flying would be negative? Why couldn't I think about some of the good experiences, which, over a career that has lasted more than half my life, far outweigh the relatively few bad ones?

I already knew that the bad things would always be with me. I just had to make sure that they didn't cause me to forget the good things.

So I started recalling the good things. The first thing that came to mind was the **Wish Flight**^{SM} trip I had worked several years earlier. It actually turned out to be the most rewarding experience of my career. The airline had put out a notice saying that they were looking for volunteers to work this special flight they had coordinated with the **something mAAgic® Foundation**, which grants the special wishes of children with life-threatening illnesses. One of the most popular wishes the foundation receives is a trip to Disney World. That year was the grand opening of the **Park of DreAAms**^{SM} playground that the airline had made a donation towards the construction of. The park is located at the Give Kids The World Village in Kissimmee just outside of Orlando. The resort is designed to provide an escape from the hospitals and treatment centers where they spend so much of their lives. Everything at the Village is handicapped-accessible. There are facilities with medical equipment to accommodate the special needs of these children and doctors are on call at all times. The families stay in little villas right inside the village, and for one night during their stay, the parents are given a babysitter and are required to go out to a dinner or a movie or something without the kids since it is probably rare that they ever get to do so at home.

I volunteered and was accepted to work the flight, which was scheduled to take off from Dallas with fifteen **Wish Flight**^{SM} families from the surrounding area to Orlando, where they would get to stay at the Village and go to Disney World. There had been an overwhelming response of flight attendants who volunteered to work this flight, so I felt truly blessed to be one of the chosen few.

I had to get up very early that morning to fly to Dallas, and when I got there I was greeted by a representative from the airline who escorted me to a conference room where the other crew members were gathered to discuss the flight procedures. The aircraft we would be using was a special Boeing 757 that had been purchased in 1992 with money contributed by American Airlines employees. During the briefing we were told that safety, as always, was our first priority, but otherwise we should make this flight as much fun as possible for the kids. We were then taken to the plane for a pre-flight walkthrough and found giant teddy bears and bags of gifts waiting for the kids on each of their seats.

After the walk through, we were led to a special waiting room decorated with ribbons and balloons where the children and their families were gathered. Players from the Dallas Stars and the Dallas Cowboys were there, as were the Cowboy cheerleaders. There were clowns, Barney the Dinosaur, face painting, cake, candy, ice cream, and all the other things that kids love. Everyone was so excited! I don't think I've ever been in a room that had so much positive energy, and I knew right then and there that this was going to be an amazing day.

When it was time to board the plane, there was a marching band that led everyone to the gate. As we were walking through the terminal, members of the press were taking pictures and the kids were made to feel like celebrities, smiling and waving for the cameras while being applauded and cheered by bystanders. The kids got even more excited after we boarded the plane. I had a moment of weakness where I started to think about how heartbreaking it was that some of them had only months to live. But that wasn't what this trip was about, so I pushed all negative thoughts aside in order to do my part to help make this one of the greatest experiences of their lives.

First class is usually the place to be during a flight, but not this time. All the corporate bigwigs sat there, as well as the doctor and the nurse. There was even a mechanic just in case we needed one. American had taken all sorts of extra precautions to ensure that this flight would be flawless. Also, one of the kids had a father who was a fireman, so arrangements had been made to have two fire trucks out on the tarmac douse the plane with hoses on either side, similar to what the mechanics do as a tribute after a captain's last flight. The kids absolutely loved it! They laughed and cheered when the water was running down the sides of the plane, and that alone brought a tear to my eye. I don't think I've ever seen a group of kids as happy as they were.

After we took off and completed our in-flight procedures, the captain opened the door to the flight deck so that the kids could come in and out of the cockpit, which was normally not permissible, but an exception was made for this flight only. The flight attendants tried to come up with fun stuff to do during the flight, and someone suggested a singing contest. We divided the kids into groups of three to see who could sing the loudest. Each group screamed the words of the song at the top of their lungs as if they were having the time of their lives, never mind that there wasn't really any actual singing going on!

The kids ranged in age from three to fifteen, and about half-hour into the flight the oldest girl, who was undergoing chemotherapy treatments, said to me, "I really don't like wearing my wig-do you mind if I take it off?"

"Of course not!" I said. "Go ahead!" I couldn't believe that this girl with life-threatening cancer was thoughtful enough to ask if I minded if she took her wig off. She thought it might make everyone on board the aircraft feel uncomfortable to see her without hair. It was so touching that I almost started crying again, but I was able to fight it off.

After landing in Orlando, the families deplaned one at a time and were greeted at the gate by a giant rabbit named Clayton, who was the mayor of the Village. There was also a marching band and a town crier who announced, "Here ye, here ye, the Give Kids the World Village welcomes the [so-and-so] family." Other characters from the Village were there as well, and each family received a round of applause after being announced and then they were escorted to the bus that would take them to the Village.

After the families were gone, the rest of the crew got back on the plane and flew back to Dallas. I could have just flown back to New York from Orlando, which would have gotten me home much sooner, but I took the long way because I didn't want the day to end. The ride back was quiet without the kids and sort of a letdown after the earlier excitement. I was glad that I got to work the flight going to Orlando rather than coming back. That must have been depressing for the kids to be flying back to their regular routines of hospital stays and medical treatments. It was truly an amazing experience, and the proudest I've ever felt as an employee of American Airlines. If I ever had the opportunity again, I would do it in a heartbeat, but, of course, that opportunity would never come if I quit.

From my deck chair overlooking the Caribbean, I recalled many more of the good times, and it seemed hard to believe how quickly the years had gone by. What moved me more than the individual memories, though, was the thought of the overall experience. I remember hearing somewhere that you should first find what you love to do and then find a way to get paid for it. That's exactly what I had done! I realized how fortunate I was to have found that when I was seven and then started getting paid for it when I was twenty-two. Combine that with a loving, supportive husband, two beautiful daughters, and all the wonderful friends I've made during my career, I've had a wonderful life.

So wonderful, in fact, that I never really gave much thought to doing anything else. Perhaps I should have thought of a backup plan, but I couldn't think of anything that I would enjoy as much as being a flight attendant. Before going to Dallas for my initial flight attendant training, I had found a job that I liked, but it wasn't something that I would have wanted to pursue as a career. After I started flying, it didn't seem necessary to find a backup plan because, now that I was on the inside, I figured I could just keep on flying until I retired. What I did after retirement was something I wasn't going to worry about until I actually got there. Now that it was staring me in the face, however, I realized that I had arrived totally unprepared.

I tried to think of something else I could do besides flying, but I couldn't come up with anything. How can anything else compare to a job where, when you leave for work, you might be having dinner in London, or going shopping in Paris, or strolling through the streets of Zurich at Christmas time, or watching a sunset in the Caribbean? It really was a dream life. There also weren't too many jobs that would allow me the same flexibility that being a flight attendant did. I had always been there for my family when they needed me-I didn't miss any major event in my daughters' lives-and, even now, if I did go back, I could work only a few trips a month if I wanted to, which wouldn't be too bad. With another job, even a part-time job, I wouldn't really have any control over when or how much I worked.

Then I started thinking about my father. What would he have thought if I quit now? I still had another four years left until retirement, and I kept hearing him say that that the job wasn't finished yet and that I still had work to do. I knew he probably would have understood if I quit now after what I had been through, but I also couldn't help thinking that he would be a little disappointed. It was his work ethic that had gotten me through more than twenty-five years of being a flight attendant, and I knew he was up there somewhere keeping an eye on me and anxiously waiting to see what I would do next. I didn't want to let him down.

Towards the end of the cruise I was out on the deck watching a sunset when I recalled a question someone had asked me recently. This person was familiar with all of my stories and all that I had been through, and the question was, "If you could turn back the clock, would you do it all over again?" Without hesitation I answered, "Yes!" I couldn't even imagine what my life would have been like if I hadn't been a flight attendant. So, if I couldn't imagine the past without flying, why was I trying to imagine the future without it?

During the cruise I hadn't mentioned to Doug that I was thinking about flying again. When we got home, however, I very casually said to him, "Oh, by the way, I'm going down to Dallas in a couple of weeks for my yearly training, and then I'm going to start flying again."

"Okay," he said. He didn't even flinch! At first I was shocked at his non-reaction because I had been expecting him to protest, but then I realized that he probably knew even before I did that I would go back eventually. Looking back now, I'm almost surprised that I hadn't realized it sooner myself. But it took me a while to peel back the layers that had been piling up over my heart since Jose died. I had difficulty looking ahead until I had done so. As soon as I had, I realized that I didn't need to do anything else because there really was nothing else. Flying was all I had ever wanted to do, and that hadn't changed despite the efforts of my grief to make me think otherwise.

While Doug didn't try to talk me out of it, Kirsten was a tougher sell. She had been relieved when I took my leave of absence and was even more relieved when I said that I was seriously considering retirement. As I knew she would, she started putting up an argument when I told her I was going back. Yet, it didn't take her long to realize that it was no use. My mind was already made up, and she knew that she wasn't going to be able to talk me out of it.

Kelly, on the other hand, not only supported my decision when she came home in May after the spring semester of her sophomore year at the University of Central Florida, she absolutely shocked us by announcing that she wanted to be a pilot. Up until then, I had no idea that she had inherited my flying gene. That was Kelly, always full of surprises. It's ironic how much she turned out to be like me despite all the battles we had when she was a teenager. I was so excited because I probably would have wanted to be a pilot too had I been born at a later time. My flying gene had manifested into a desire to become a flight attendant because I had never heard of women pilots when I was a little girl (Amelia Earhart was well before my time), so the thought never even occurred to me until later in life. I have actually taken a few flying lessons for fun and loved it. I guess I was just born too soon. But I was so happy for Kelly and so proud of her that I didn't dwell too long on my own disappointment of not having that option presented to me when I was her age.

While she was still down at U.C.F., she had applied to the Embry Riddle Aeronautical College in Daytona without telling anyone about it until she was accepted a few months later for the upcoming fall 2002 semester. After finally telling us about this, she then dropped her next bombshell-she had also applied for a summer job with North American Airlines, a relatively new carrier that had held most of the military personnel transport contracts. Out of several hundred people who applied for the position, she was one of nineteen people who was hired.

"Hired to do what?" I asked.

"I'm going to be a flight attendant!"

I nearly fainted on the spot. While I was very proud of her and happy that she had finally found something she really wanted to do, I was alarmed that being a flight attendant was going to interfere with her goal of becoming a pilot. I knew full well that once being a flight attendant gets in your blood, it is very difficult to give up. If she discovered that she could fly all over the world without having to put all that effort into learning how to pilot an aircraft, I was afraid that she might just give up on that goal and continue working as a flight attendant.

My concern was justified when she decided at the end of the summer that she wanted to keep on flying as a flight attendant since

Embry Riddle was willing to hold her spot open until the following fall. She was having the time of her life traveling to places I had only dreamed of ever visiting-Saudi Arabia, Bahrain, and Kuwait, to name a few. While I was happy that she was getting the experience of a lifetime, I was also very worried because some of these places weren't exactly hospitable towards Americans, especially at a time when tensions were rising in the Gulf region as talk of an attack on Iraq started growing louder. I became really alarmed in October when a U.S. Marine was killed by terrorists in Kuwait while she was staying there. I took my concern out on Doug since he encouraged her to see what the airline industry was like before committing herself to becoming a pilot. I would have preferred if she had just found a typical summer job at home and went straight to Embry Riddle in the fall.

"If something happens to her, I'll never forgive you!" I said to him after hearing the news about the Marine.

"Jean, think back," he said calmly. "What would you do if your mother told you that she didn't want you flying anywhere?"

I thought about it for a minute.

"You're right," I said. "I probably would have told her to take a flying leap."

Kelly e-mailed us from Bahrain and told us that everything was fine and not to worry. They were receiving security briefings every day. That is what made me feel a little better. When she did eventually get home, she admitted that she was apprehensive when they first arrived in Kuwait and when they were going through Customs. She immediately sensed that Americans were not well-liked. Therefore, her layover was spent in her hotel room and swimming in the Mediterranean.

That was the only time she felt uncomfortable overseas, however, and she said that the rest of it was absolutely amazing. She spent her twentieth birthday in Greece, which was the first time I had not been with one of my daughters on her birthday. This was a very sad day for me.

"Do you think it bothers her to be so far from her parents on her birthday?" I asked Doug.

"Let's see," he said. "She's young, she's beautiful, she's in Crete surrounded by military men-I don't think she even knows that she has parents!"

I understood what he was saying, but I still just had to talk to her. I attempted to find out where she was staying by calling the crew scheduler at North American Airlines. As is standard procedure for most airlines, however, the woman I spoke to would not divulge what hotel she was staying at.

"Listen," I said. "I work for an airline myself and I am very familiar with that policy. But today is my daughter's twentieth birthday, and if you don't think I'm going to find some way to get in touch with her, you've got another thing coming! So why don't you just save me the trouble and tell me where she is!" She must have been a mother too because, while she wouldn't tell me the name of the hotel, she did give me the phone number, so I was able to call and wish her a happy birthday.

Finally in December, to my great relief, Kelly resigned from North American Airlines. She also changed her mind about becoming a pilot and decided to go back to U.C.F. in January, which meant that she would have only missed one semester of school. At first I was a little disappointed that she wasn't going to become a pilot, but I was so proud of her when she still managed to graduate on time a year and a half later with a bachelor's degree in criminal justice and a minor in Mid-Eastern studies that she added after returning from her adventures overseas.

After completing my yearly training down in Dallas, I finally went back to work following an eight month leave of absence. To my surprise, the difficult part was not so much getting used to the routine of flying again as much as having to adjust to how much the industry had changed during the time I was out. In the two months following September 11, the government had started to implement changes in security procedures, but that was only the beginning. The industry itself had changed drastically with all the major airlines making huge cutbacks in trying to stay out of bankruptcy and competing with upstart economy airlines. These cutbacks resulted in longer hours and smaller paychecks, which had many veteran flight attendants starting to count the days until they were eligible for retirement and hoping and that their pensions would still be awaiting them when they got there.

Every day, it is becoming more and more difficult to make a living as a flight attendant. The job itself is becoming less tolerable. It seems that every time you go to work there is some new security procedure, or service cutback, or rumor of bankruptcy. With fuel prices on the rise and customers unwilling to pay higher ticket prices, it is probably only going to keep getting worse. Sometimes it feels like there's a death watch for all the old major airlines, and, when you see all these upstarts succeeding with their barebones service and their crews not being paid much more than minimum wage, it makes you a little sentimental for the old days. I am beginning to wonder if in the very near future, flying won't be that much different than riding a bus.

Still, this is where I belong. In fact, maybe all the changes were good for me because I was so busy adjusting to them that I didn't feel surrounded by constant reminders of tragedy. There are still reminders, but they are mostly on the calendar, not on the airplane. For instance, I have not and will not fly on November 20, the anniversary of Jose's death, and every year I send Jose's mother flowers or a card to let her know that he has not been forgotten. I also will not fly on November 12, the anniversary of the crash of flight 587 (November is a rough month). I will, however, fly on September 11. I feel it is important not to allow terrorists to alter my flight schedule. It is still sad to fly over New York on that day and see that stunning view of the Manhattan skyline without seeing the Twin Towers.

Then there's New Year's Eve, the anniversary of my hijacking. I have not flown on December 31 since 1984, and every year Doug and I commemorate the event by taking a drink of Cuban rum. The date, however, isn't the only reminder of that night. Not long after it happened, I had one of those revelations that many people have following a near-death experience about how it is important to live for the moment because you never know when your life is going to end. My revelation actually worked out quite well for Doug because he loves boats but hadn't owned one in a while. I suggested to him that he buy one before the upcoming summer provided that we didn't have to take out any loans to pay for it. "Live for today!" I said to him. After realizing that I wasn't kidding, he went out and bought a 21 foot Bay liner. It wasn't until afterwards that I started to think, *what's wrong with this picture? If I'm the one who got hijacked and almost lost my life, how is it that he's the one who wound up with a new boat?*

Doug, to his credit, at least acknowledged the source of his good fortune in the naming of the boat, but he wouldn't tell me what it was until the little christening ceremony we had down at the marina prior to its maiden voyage. When we got to the dock, the name that had been painted on the back of the boat was covered by a tarp, and Doug prolonged the suspense by giving a little speech. Finally, after I couldn't take it anymore, he pulled the tarp away and I just stared at the name in stunned silence. I didn't know what to think at first, but my husband's unmistakable wit eventually got the better of me and I started laughing.

He had named the boat *Hijacked.*

Now here I am two years away from retirement, and, when that time comes, I think I'll finally be ready to turn in my wings. I don't think I'll be tired of flying by then, but I will probably be too tired to keep working as a flight attendant because of the long hours we are now required to put in. The cutbacks have gotten to the point where the airlines no longer want to pay for flight attendants to stay at hotels. Where in the past we would have had a nice layover, they now have us take a quick break and then put us right back on the plane to work a turnaround flight. Turnarounds used to be only done for three and four hour flights, but now they are being done for six or seven hour flights that result in twelve to fourteen hour days that are absolutely exhausting. I realize that things like this have to be done in order for the airlines to survive, but that doesn't make it any easier for someone who has been flying as long as I have to accept. Forget about glamour- this job has become a plain old grind!

Yet, as difficult as it has become, I still love to fly, and I have welcomed the challenge presented before me. I still don't know what I'm going to do after I retire, but as long as I finish my career in full, I know the decision won't be so pressing and I will have no guilt as I surely would feel if I retired early. Perhaps I will just keep on flying as a passenger and visit some of the places I didn't get to see over my career. Maybe I'll do some volunteer work for my favorite charities, or maybe I'll be struck by divine inspiration to do something I haven't thought of yet. Right now I just don't know, but I'm not going to worry about it at the moment because I still have some work to do before then. Maybe I'll even write a book!

12.

Paco Goes Haywire

Of course, I can't expect to just fly off into the sunset without encountering a little more turbulence...

In May 2004, I had been assigned the number one position on a Boeing 777 from London to New York and was working in the first class section when, Mike, the galley flight attendant, called me from the back of the plane and said, "Jean, there's a problem-you have to come back here!"

My first thought was, *Where have I heard that before?* but there was an urgency in his voice that quickly made me realize that the situation was probably serious.

"What's the problem?" I asked, trying to remain calm, but the adrenaline was already starting to kick in. After all I have been through in my nearly three decades of flying, it is amazing that my adrenal glands haven't dried up by now! And, not only do they still work, since 9/11 it seems these glands have started producing an especially potent form of adrenaline in flight attendants that, once it starts surging through your body, makes you realize that you would do just about anything to ensure the safety of the plane and everyone on board.

"I'm having a problem with a passenger!" Mike said. "You have to come back here quickly!"

"I'm on my way."

The 777 is a big plane, so it took me a couple of minutes to get all the way to the back from first class. When I did finally get there, I saw this really large young man standing in the galley in front of Mike. He was talking rapidly and didn't make any sense. The man looked in my direction as I approached, but he had this strange look in his eyes that made it seem like he wasn't really seeing what was in front of him. In fact, he seemed to be looking at something else entirely with an expression of angry bewilderment. Beads of sweat were running down his face and his body was trembling slightly. Although he didn't appear to have a gun or some other kind of weapon with which he was threatening Mike, I couldn't just assume that he was unarmed. I also had to keep in mind that this might be some kind of ploy to distract the crew while something else was happening in another section of the aircraft.

I stopped several feet short of the galley and asked the man what the problem was. At first he didn't seem to hear me or even notice that I was there, but then he suddenly came out of his trance and shouted, "I am not an American!"

His eruption startled me and I jumped back a couple of feet. Despite his claim, his accent very clearly indicated that he was an American.

"Please don't shout, sir," I said after I had regained my composure.

"Don't stereotype me!" he said, waving his index finger at me.

"Okay, sir," I said. "I won't stereotype you. I just need to know what the problem is."

Suddenly he turned to Mike and shouted, "I hate you, Mother!" Mike assumed a defensive posture as if about to be struck, but the man slipped back into his own little world and started muttering under his breath. I couldn't understand what he was saying, but he almost appeared to be talking to someone else by the way he would occasionally pause as if awaiting a response. I looked at Mike hoping that maybe he could shed some light on the situation, but he looked just as confused and frightened as I was.

"He thinks I'm his mother," he said, and suddenly the man erupted and started yelling at me again.

"I hate you, Mother! Why didn't you leave him? I hate you, you bitch!"

Just as suddenly as he had snapped, he went right back to his muttering. Mike carefully stepped away from him in order to talk to me so that he wouldn't overhear us.

"A few minutes ago he thought I was his therapist," he whispered. "Saying the wrong thing seems to set him off."

"Is he alone?" I asked.

"No, he's with his girlfriend-she's sitting over there."

Mike pointed out the girlfriend to me, which the man noticed.

"She thinks I'm going to marry her!" he shouted. "But I'm not! I don't believe in the institution of marriage!"

"Sir!" I said. "I'm going to have to ask you to stop shouting and please go back to your seat!"

Again he drifted away and started muttering.

"Do you know his name?" I whispered to Mike.

"He said his name is 'Paco.' He mentioned the name before, so I asked him who Paco was, and he said that he was Paco and then he started swearing and rambling on about how he wanted to kill his father. Jean, this guy has lost his mind!"

While we were talking, a man got up out of his seat and headed down the aisle across from where we were standing and disappeared into the galley, which has a lavatory on either side. I didn't pay much attention to him until he reappeared on the opposite side of the galley behind Paco and stood outside one of the lavatory doors as if waiting to use it even though the 'occupied' sign was not illuminated. This made me very suspicious, and when he noticed me looking at him over Paco's shoulder, he reached for something in his pocket. I thought he might be pulling out a gun, but, to my great relief, he held up an American Airlines crew badge and mouthed the word 'deadheader,' this meant that he was an off-duty flight attendant. I gave him a nod to indicate that I understood, Paco must have noticed because he turned around and started screaming at him.

"I hate you, Father!" he yelled. "I should kill you!" He then turned to me and yelled, "Why didn't you leave him? How could you not leave him after what he did to me? *He's* the one who needed therapy, but I'm the one spending half my life talking to therapists!" He then turned and pointed at me. "And you-you're the only good therapist I've ever had! Tell them there's nothing wrong with me! Tell them that I'm not the aggressor! Tell them that I'm the victim!"

"Paco!" I said, and for the first time I had his attention. "Why don't we sit down and talk about it. I'm sure that we can straighten this out."

"Yes," he said. "Let's talk. *You* know there's nothing wrong with me. You're the only one who understands!"

At this point, I knew that he was under the impression that I was his therapist and that this impression seemed to have a calming affect on him. I also understood that this man did not seem to be a terrorist and that it was probably not his intention to endanger the safety of the aircraft or anyone on board, yet that is exactly what his erratic behavior was doing. I knew I had to be very careful about everything I said.

Fortunately, the flight was not full, so the last several rows of seats were empty. Economy seating in a Boeing 777 is set up in a 2-5-2 configuration, meaning that there are two seats on either side of the aircraft next to the windows and five in the middle. I had Paco sit in the middle seat of the middle section, while another female flight attendant sat on one side of him and I sat on the other. Our thinking was that having him sit between us would make it more difficult for him to get up, but he was a big enough guy to easily overpower us if he really wanted to.

After I was seated, I was momentarily reminded of that night twenty years earlier when I was sitting in the back of a DC-10 with a certain hijacker. I knew then that if I said the wrong thing, I could get myself and everyone else on the plane killed. I was once again placed in a similar situation because who knew what this guy would do if I were to say something to set him off. Oddly enough, dealing with the hijacker almost seemed easier in a way. He at least specifically stated what he wanted us to do and we didn't have any r choice but to comply; the man I was sitting next to now was either in the process of losing his mind or had already lost it. What he wanted was not only unclear to us; it was probably also unclear to him. He may not have even been aware that he was sitting on an airplane, so it was nearly impossible to have a rational conversation with him. His unpredictability made him dangerous, so I thought that our best chance of keeping the situation under control was to let him think that I was his psychiatrist and to go along with whatever else he might say until we were safely back on the ground. Since we were still four or five hours outside of New York, however, this seemed like a daunting task.

"So, Paco," I said, "Why don't you tell me a little about yourself."

"Get away from me, Mother!" he shouted at me. "Go away!"

I quickly got out of my seat, and his agitation subsided as soon as I had done so. The other flight attendant started talking to him and he now thought that she was the therapist and I was the mother. I stood in the aisle for a moment trying to figure out what to do next when I noticed the young woman who had been identified as Paco's girlfriend looking back at us. I asked one of the other flight attendants if she would sit down next to Paco where I had been sitting so I could go talk to the girlfriend and try to find out a little more about him. I waited until she was seated to make sure that her presence didn't set him off, but he didn't seem to notice her because the other flight attendant was talking to him and had his attention for the moment.

The girlfriend was an adorable young lady who looked like the girl next door. Although at this point I was confident that the two of them were not working together to sabotage the flight, I still had to remain cautious and not make any assumptions.

"You have to tell me about your boyfriend back there," I said. "Paco-that's his name, right?"

"Yes," she said. She looked like she was about to start crying. "I don't know what's wrong with him. I've been dating him for four years, but nothing like this has ever happened. He's never acted like this before."

"Has he been taking any drugs?" I asked.

"No."

"He's not on heroin? Cocaine? LSD?"

"No!"

"Has he ever taken drugs?"

"We smoke pot together once in a while."

"When was the last time he smoked pot?"

"A couple of weeks ago."

"What about alcohol?"

"He hardly ever drinks."

"Has he been drinking today?"

"No."

She seemed to be telling the truth, which pretty much confirmed my suspicion that Paco's behavior was the symptom of a mental disorder and not some form of inebriation. I had dealt with passengers under the influence of drugs and alcohol in the past, and none of them had ever had an outburst quite like Paco's.

"Alright then," I said. "What's the story here? What were you doing in Europe?"

"Teaching English," she said. "We were both teaching English in Paris, and we just spent the last two weeks traveling around Europe. He was very upset about the war in Iraq, and he was very upset about the anti-Americanism in Paris and in the rest of France-all over Europe really-and then he just snapped."

"Did something specific happen to trigger this?"

"No, not really. I think it just started to build up and then he exploded. He started acting like this last night and I thought maybe he would be better in the morning, but he wasn't." She was crying now. "I called his parents and they told me to get him on a plane immediately and that they would take care of him when we got home."

"Oh, terrific," I said. "You know, you really should have let somebody know that he was having a problem before he got on the plane. Now this has become a problem for everyone on this aircraft."

"I'm sorry. I just didn't know what else to do!"

We talked a little longer and she told me that they were both twenty-three and that Paco was considered brilliant with a high I.Q. He had recently graduated from Princeton. She also mentioned that when he was a child, he had been molested by his father, but, even though his mother knew about what her husband had done, she did not leave him. Paco hated her for staying and had been in therapy for years, yet he seemed to have been dealing with it just fine and it was hardly an issue until now. The antagonism they encountered abroad had apparently really bothered him. The Europeans didn't seem to care that he felt the same way they did about the war in Iraq; all they seemed to notice was that he was an American, which, in their eyes, automatically made him guilty. This may have triggered the scene he was now living out in the back of the plane, the innocent child being attacked for reasons that were no fault of his own. I felt terrible for both of them having to go through this and realized that, if I were in her shoes, I probably wouldn't have known what to do either. I had to push my sympathy aside and deal with the situation at hand.

I decided to move her to a seat in a different section of the aircraft where Paco wouldn't be able to see her since the sight of her earlier had upset him, and then I was going to try to find a doctor. I recruited one of the other flight attendants to help me go to each section of the aircraft and personally ask the passengers rather than using the P.A. system. I was afraid that Paco might become agitated if he heard us asking for a doctor.

I went up to first class and had started asking the passengers if any of them were doctors when the captain called me. He had already been given a quick assessment of the situation, but he wanted to talk to me.

"I don't believe that he's a terrorist or that his aim is to hurt anyone," I told him. "Basically, I think he just snapped. It sounds like he's been through a lot, and it just got to be a little too much for him and he went over the edge."

He radioed American Airlines headquarters in Dallas, where there is a doctor on call at all times in case of in-flight medical emergencies and explained the situation. Unfortunately, the doctor said that he wasn't qualified to handle something such as this and that we would need to talk to a psychiatrist. He asked us to stand by while he got in touch with one. After he had, the captain and I explained the situation once more. I told the psychiatrist that we were trying to find a doctor on board and suggested that if we even found a nurse, maybe we could inject him with valium since he was posing a threat to the safety of the aircraft.

"Absolutely not!" he said. "You cannot go near him with a needle while he's in a psychotic state. He will only become even more agitated."

"What if we find some big passengers who can hold him down while we handcuff him—"

"Absolutely not!" he said again. "That is out of the question-don't even try it!"

"What are we supposed to do then?"

"Just do your best to keep him calm as you've been doing."

This was not what I wanted to hear, and, judging by the expression on my face, the captain knew it. After signing off with the psychiatrist, he looked up at me and said, "Jean, I need to know if we can continue all the way to New York like this."

"I don't know," I said. "I mean, he's a big guy and he could overpower us if he really wanted to, but he hasn't tried to do that yet. I guess we could just do what we've been doing and go along with whatever he says, but I don't know if that's going to work for another four or five hours. It's pretty exhausting."

"Well, here's the situation. Right now we have a ten minute window where we can divert to Iceland. If that window closes, we're going to New York."

"I don't know. We've managed to keep him fairly calm doing what we're doing, but if he really loses it, I don't know what would happen. I just don't know."

Just then the phone rang and the captain answered.

"Tell Jean she has to get back here!" It was Mickey. "The guy is really going crazy and he's looking for her!"

"That's it!" the captain said. "We're going to Iceland. We'll be there in about an hour."

After leaving the cockpit, the flight attendant who had been looking for a doctor informed me that she had found a nurse and a man who said he was a mental health professional. I thanked her and asked her to go around and explain to the passengers that we were diverting to Reykjavik and to tell them why. Also to tell them that when the captain made the P.A. announcement, he was going to say that we were landing in New York because we were worried that Paco might react badly if he found out we were going elsewhere.

We didn't need the nurse since we wouldn't be administering any shots, so I quickly explained to the mental health professional what was going on and asked him to come to the back. I also recruited a military man who volunteered to help us out just in case Paco really lost it.

"Mother!" Paco screamed when he saw me coming down the aisle. He was standing up in the seat with fists clenched pounding on the back of the seat in front of him. "I hate you, Mother!"

"But I love you, Paco," I said as sweetly as I could.

That stopped him for a moment and he looked at me quizzically.

"How can you love me?" he asked. "How can you say that you love me after I just told you that I hate you?"

"Because that's the way mothers are," I said. I then turned around and asked the mental health professional what his name was, and he said it was 'Michael.'

"Paco," I said, "this is my friend Michael. He would like to sit down and talk to you if that's okay."

The other flight attendant got up to let Michael sit down, but he never had a chance. When Paco saw him, he mistook him for his father and went into a rage. Michael tried talking to him, but Paco didn't seem to hear anything he said.

"Jean, this guy is ticking him off even more," Mike said worriedly.

"Yes, I can see that," I said. I went over to Michael and tapped him on the shoulder.

"Michael," I said, "I think I would like to talk to Paco now."

"That's probably a good idea," he said. The other flight attendant suggested to Michael that he go into the galley so that he would be able to listen to what Paco was saying and possibly offer some advice as we went along.

Paco calmed down again after Michael was gone, and I managed to convince him to sit back down. I spoke with my sweet voice and asked him if there was anything he'd like to talk about, but he was already back in his own little world. That was perfectly fine with me, and I was hoping he would stay there until we landed. I didn't want to say or do anything that might agitate him, and fortunately the others were thinking the same thing and stayed out of sight.

In the meantime, the rest of the crew had stepped right in to cover for those of us who were dealing with Paco and kept the passengers away by directing them to the lavatories in the middle and front of the aircraft. Often in this job, you don't really know how good your fellow crew members are at what they do until something happens. Having been given the opportunity, this crew absolutely shined. Their coordination made the situation much less difficult than it could have been. They did a wonderful job of covering for us and keeping the rest of the passengers calm by explaining that there was a man in desperate need of medical attention without emphasizing that this same man was a risk to everyone on board that aircraft. I'm sure some of the passengers were frustrated about the delay, but hardly anyone complained.

Paco was calm for the most part during the rest of the flight, but he did jump up a couple of times and started screaming incoherently until we managed to talk him into sitting back down. The others kept a close watch from the galley and were ready to help subdue him if necessary, but it never came to that. As noisy as he was, Paco was relatively harmless, and more than anything, I just felt sorry for him.

A short time later, the captain made the announcement that we would be landing in New York, and Paco didn't offer any reaction to this. The others in the galley quietly seated themselves nearby trying not to attract Paco's attention. While he did momentarily become agitated when he saw them, he did not jump up and start screaming. I told him that he had to buckle his seatbelt because we would be landing soon, and I buckled my own hoping that he would follow my example, which he did. He was quiet for the rest of the flight, but, after we had safely touched down, I became very concerned about what was going to happen next.

I knew the authorities would be waiting at the gate, and my hope was that they would approach calmly rather than storming onto the aircraft. I had a feeling that Paco was not going to react well when he saw them. After the plane had rolled to a stop, the captain made an announcement asking the passengers to remain seated, and we sat there quietly for a couple of minutes. Since I was the purser on the flight, I was actually supposed to be in my jumpseat for landing but I had stayed with Paco in the back of the airplane. One of the other flight attendants took over my jumpseat position.

I waited anxiously until I heard a commotion in the section ahead of us, and I knew the authorities were storming towards us. I quickly unbuckled my seatbelt and hurried down the aisle hoping to cut them off before Paco saw them and warn them to approach calmly. I encountered the first police officer and stopped him. There were several other police officers and men in white coats behind him.

"What's your name?" I asked the officer.

"Peter," he said.

"Okay Peter, I'm going to ask you to remain calm because our friend back there is easily agitated. His name is Paco. So, if you'll just follow me in a nice, calm manner, I will lead you to him. Okay?"

"Okay," Peter said.

I slowly led Peter towards the back until we arrived at the last row.

Paco had his head down and was muttering to himself, so he didn't notice me until I sat back down next to him.

"Paco," I said with my motherly voice. "This is my friend Peter. I want you to say hi to my friend Peter."

He looked up at Peter and then at all the men lined up in the aisle behind him, and I realized from his expression that he was about to explode. I quickly stood up and dove over the back of the seat in front of me just as Paco let out one of the loudest screams I've ever heard. He struggled to get up and get away, but he still had his seatbelt on. This made it difficult for the police to subdue him because they first had to unbuckle the belt and then try to restrain him once he had been freed. It took about ten men to finally get him under control, and, as they were removing him from the plane, he kept yelling to me and the other flight attendant, "Don't let them take me!" It was such a sad sight that she and I both started to cry, but we were also relieved that we were now out of danger.

In the meantime, Paco's girlfriend had asked the flight attendant who had told the other passengers that we were diverting to Reykjavik if she would be able to get off the plane and stay with him. We weren't sure if that would be possible as that decision was probably going to have to be made by the authorities in Iceland. She was told to gather her belongings just in case they decided to let her stay, which they ultimately did.

I don't know what ever happened to Paco after he was taken off our plane, but I truly hope he received and is still receiving the help that he needs. I also hope that the authorities treated him not like a criminal but as an individual in desperate need of help. Someone who causes a disruption on a commercial airliner to that extreme in the post-9/11 world is not likely to be treated with kid gloves.

After he was gone, I thought we would have to spend the night in Iceland. The cockpit crew was about to run out of flight hours, and, if they did, they would not be able to initiate another flight before taking a mandatory rest break. I was so convinced of it that I started looking forward to a nice fresh fish dinner at a restaurant in Reykjavik, but the ground crew quickly refueled the plane and sent us back out to the runway. We were already in the air as time expired.

The crew was exhausted, and I thanked them for the wonderful job they did and also thanked the military man and Michael, the mental health professional, for helping out. I apologized to Michael for relieving him when it became clear that his presence was agitating Paco even more, but he said I had done the right thing.

"You did a fabulous job," he said. "You just rolled right with it. Me being there only made it worse because it was obvious that he could not relate to a male figure."

"I only wish I had said something before we took off in London," the military man said. "Before boarding the plane, I was in the men's room in the lounge washing my hands when I heard this guy talking. I didn't think anything of it at first because I thought he was talking to someone else, so I didn't even look up. But he was saying some pretty strange things. I finally looked up and saw in the mirror that he was alone. Then I thought he was talking to me, but he didn't even seem to know I was there."

"You should have told someone!" I said angrily. "You should always say something when you see something strange at an airport! If you had, this whole thing could have been avoided!"

While I was driving home later that night, I just had to laugh. "What's going to happen next?" I said out loud. "What could possibly happen next?"

Right now I can't even imagine, but I'm sure it'll be something that will once again challenge my will to continue flying and cause me to ask myself why I continue to do it.

Yet, I still think that the biggest challenge will come after I turn in my wings. It will be hard not to put on the uniform anymore and not plan my monthly calendar around what trips are available. I know I'll still fly as a passenger and still go to the monthly luncheons and so forth, but I am worried that these things will only make me realize how much I miss it. I know there will be a terrible sadness when I finally wake up from this dream I've been having since I was seven years old, a dream so wild and crazy and beautiful that I might have a hard time convincing myself that it was actually real.

Endnotes

* According the N.T.S.B. Safety Recommendation Report, the cabin altimeter indicated an altitude of 19,000 feet during flight 1291's approach to MIA, but the actual air pressure in the cabin corresponded to an altitude of *negative* 12,500 feet. Because the altimeter only measures altitudes down to -5,000 feet, the needle on the gauge (which was a circular instrument like a clock face) circled back around to a reading of positive 19,000 feet, which is why the captain thought the plane was depressurizing even though it was already over pressurized to the point where the smoke alarms started going off, the phones and passenger call bells started ringing, and people started complaining that their ears were beginning to hurt.

The report states: "When cabin pressure increases such that the cabin altitude is less than -5,000 feet, the cabin altimeter needle moves counterclockwise through the negative altitude range, including past the -5,000 mark, through the unmarked area, and into the highest end of the positive altitude range... because the cabin altimeter's negative range stops at -5,000 feet, the -12,100 foot cabin altitude would have registered on the cabin altimeter in the high end of the positive range, indicating a cabin altitude of 19,000 feet. This would have presented the flight crew with a misleading indication of a high cabin altitude (indicating low cabin pressure) when, in fact, the cabin was pressurized well above ambient pressure."

* The N.T.S.B. states the following in the Probable Cause Report regarding the explosion of TWA flight 800 on 7/17/96: "An explosion of the center wing fuel tank (CWT), resulting from the ignition of the flammable fuel/air mixture in the tank. The source of ignition energy for the explosion could not be determined with certainty, but, of the sources evaluated by the investigation, the most likely was a short circuit outside of the CWT that allowed excessive voltage to enter it through electrical wiring associated with the fuel quantity indication system." This assessment, however, has been challenged by many who

believe that flight 800 was actually shot down by a missile, and that the N.T.S.B. was ordered by high-ranking government officials in office at the time to find an alternate explanation for the explosion, which was ultimately attributed to faulty wiring.

* The N.T.S.B.'s "Brief of Accident" report states that shortly after American Airlines flight 587 took off from JFK on 11/12/01, "The airplane's vertical stabilizer and rudder separated in flight and were found in Jamaica Bay, about 1 mile north of the main wreckage site. The airplane's engines subsequently separated in flight and were found several blocks north and east of the main wreckage site. All 260 people aboard the plane and 5 people on the ground were killed, and the airplane was destroyed by impact forces and a post crash fire." Evidence of terrorism was not found.

Made in the USA